# GRILLING

Quarto.com

First Published in 2025 by The Harvard Common Press,
an imprint of The Quarto Group,
100 Cummings Center, Suite 265-D,
Beverly, MA 01915, USA.
T (978) 282-9590 F (978) 283-2742

The Harvard Common Press titles are also available at
discount for retail, wholesale, promotional, and bulk
purchase. For details, contact the Special Sales Manager
by email at specialsales@quarto.com or by mail at
The Quarto Group, Attn: Special Sales Manager, 100
Cummings Center, Suite 265-D, Beverly, MA 01915, USA.

29 28 27 26 25      1 2 3 4 5

ISBN: 978-0-7603-9747-3

Digital edition published in 2025
eISBN: 978-0-7603-9748-0

Library of Congress Cataloging-in-Publication Data

Names: Harvard Common Press, editor.
Title: Grilling / editors of the Harvard Common Press.
Description: Beverly, MA, USA : Harvard Common Press,
2025. | Series: The
    time-pressed cook | Cover title. | Includes
bibliographical references
    and index. | Summary: "In 50 inventive recipes and
dozens of useful tips
    and tricks, Grilling elevates outdoor cooking beyond
the burgers and
    dogs rut"-- Provided by publisher.
Identifiers: LCCN 2024054204 | ISBN 9780760397473
(hardcover) | ISBN
    9780760397480 (ebook)
Subjects: LCSH: Barbecuing.
Classification: LCC TX840.B3 G74927 2025 | DDC
641.5/784--dc23/eng/20241205
LC record available at https://lccn.loc.gov/2024054204

Design and Page Layout: Megan Jones Design
Photography: Joyce Oudkerk Pool, with assistance from
    Cody Gantz, except for Shutterstock on pages 7, 9,
    10–11, and 12
Illustration: Michael Korfhage

Printed in China

# GRILLING

## EDITORS OF THE HARVARD COMMON PRESS

HARVARD
COMMON
PRESS

# CONTENTS

## 1
### BEEF, PORK, AND LAMB

## 2
### CHICKEN AND DUCK

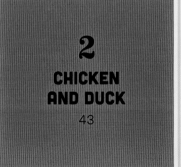

# INTRODUCTION: GRILLING BASICS

Grilling—cooking food over hot coals or flames or gas-fired burners—is done everywhere, worldwide. It is the classic method of cooking food with fire. Practiced for thousands of years, basic grilling delivers rich, uncomplicated flavor.

The goal of this book is to show you a wide variety of grilling techniques applied on a wide variety of foods. Along the way, you'll also learn how to use a rub, a marinade, a baste, or a glaze; how to manage flare-ups; how to grill and glaze bone-in chicken or pork without burning it; and how to get a steak just the way you like it, whether it's tender and juicy with good grill marks, has a smoky flavor, or is charry-crusted. You'll learn how to use your grill to grill bake a casserole, grill roast a whole chicken, or flash grill a boneless chicken breast on a busy night.

The techniques and recipes in this book are strong on simple flavors, with minimal extra seasonings. We believe that too much seasoning overpowers food's natural flavors. To our mind, the smoky flavor of charcoal and a simple sprinkle of salt and pepper are all that grilled food really needs; however, a finishing sauce, flavored butter, relish, or chutney can add color and variety.

Whether your grill is a basic charcoal kettle or a gourmet stainless-steel gas grill with all the bells and whistles, you can learn how to achieve acclaimed Memphis-style grilled ribs or a planked salmon fillet that will be the envy of your neighbors. It's all in how you manage the fire and add flavor.

So, let's get started!

## THE ESSENTIALS OF GRILLING

Grilling is a hot and fast method of cooking food directly over hot coals or flames using gas, wood, charcoal, or charcoal briquets as fuel.

### The Many Flavors of Grilling

The fantastic flavors of grilling come from three sources:

**Before grilling:** Seasonings and marinades offer zest to food before they even get to the fire.

**During grilling:** Many flavors and textures result from the grilling process itself. We're all familiar with the charry "grill marks" on our chicken breasts or burgers that result from the caramelization of the sugars in foods over high heat. In addition, smoky flavors from charcoal or wood chips, sweet and sour seasonings from barbecue sauce, or the woody aromatic taste from a wood plank are all flavors that can be added to food while it is over the flames.

**After grilling:** Finishing sauces, butters, or chutneys added after the food is removed from the fire can also greatly enhance its flavors.

## Basic Toolkit for Grillers

You can grill in brick pits, offset fireboxes, grills made from 55-gallon (209 L) drums, hibachis, improvised campfire grills, and various other grills. For many of you, your grill of choice is a standard charcoal kettle grill. Gas grills are great when you're in a hurry. The recipes in this book work for any type of grill you might have.

Once you have your grill of choice, it's time to make sure you have all the essential tools.

- **Sharp knives:** A sharp standard butcher knife is essential for trimming or slicing. Get the best you can afford. Check local restaurant supply stores for bargains on good-quality used knives.

- **Cutting boards:** We recommend boards made of hardwood or bamboo. Try to have at least two cutting boards—one for meat and one for fruits and vegetables. Thoroughly clean the cutting board between uses.

- **Long-handled fork:** Keep one handy for when tongs won't do.

- **Long-handled tongs:** Stainless-steel spring-loaded tongs work best. They are useful for spreading or moving hot coals in the grill, in addition to handling food on the grill.

- **Long-handled spatula:** A wide, long-handled spatula is especially handy for turning burgers, breads, and sliced vegetables such as eggplant.

- **Grill thermometer:** Unless you prefer to guess, use a thermometer to monitor cooking temperatures when grilling with the lid on. We recommend a candy thermometer in a vent hole at the top of the kettle lid, hooked on with baling wire attached to the handle. Higher-end gas grills come with built-in thermometers.

- **Meat thermometer:** When in doubt, use a reliable thermometer. Check standard charts for doneness temperatures.

- **Welder's gloves:** Leather welder's gloves, available in hardware stores or online, will protect your hands from the heat of the cooker. Wear them when dumping hot coals from the charcoal chimney to your bottom grate (also known as the fire grate), when brushing a grill over hot coals, and at all other times when your hands are near fire.

- **Charcoal chimney (for charcoal grills):** This is the fire-starting method of choice for most experienced cooks. See "Building the Fire" (page 13) for how to use one of these inexpensive and durable aluminized-steel starters.

- **Electric charcoal starters:** These are also popular, especially in places where smoke from burning newspaper is objectionable.

- **Perforated metal grill toppers:** When you're grilling foods small enough to slip through the grates, use a grill topper. Some are disposable, designed for just one use; others are made to last. Keep them clean.

- **Optional tools and gadgets:** Some cooks regard these optional tools and gadgets as essential: aprons, hats, aluminum foil, grill woks, fish baskets, metal skewers or kebab baskets, clean brick pavers, grill rails, a small bucket of sand for putting out grease fires, a wooden-handled dish mop, and flippers such as the PigTail.

## Building the Fire

For each recipe, you'll need to start a fire in your grill for either direct grilling (the food in direct contact with the heat) or indirect grilling (the food off to the side of the heat).

Place your charcoal chimney on a nonflammable surface and fill the top of the chimney to the desired level with briquets. Slightly tip the chimney over and stuff one to two sheets of crumpled newspaper in the convex-shaped bottom. Light the paper with a match and place the chimney on your bottom grill grate. In 15 to 20 minutes, your briquets should be glowing, ashed over, and ready to spread over the bottom of the grill.

Use lighter fluid or pretreated briquets as a last resort, and make sure coals are free of lighter residue before grilling.

For a gas grill, simply turn on the gas and set the temperature—usually medium-high. For direct grilling, turn on all the burners. For indirect grilling, leave one or two burners off, depending on how your gas grill is configured. Now you gas grillers are ready to go!

### CHARCOAL CHIMNEY TIP

To avoid the danger of dumping hot coals from your chimney, here's a tip: Remove the wires at the bottom of the chimney that separate newspaper from briquets. Load and light as usual and place in the bottom of your charcoal grill. When the coals are ready, lift the chimney, and the coals automatically fall into the bottom of the grill.

## Managing the Fire

Learning to manage your fire will allow you to increase what you can do on your grill and produce food grilled the way you want it. If something is grilling too fast and beginning to burn—the most common problem for beginners—there are several adjustments you can make to correct the problem. One is to spread the coals to one side in a charcoal grill or turn a burner off on a gas grill to create a cooler side where you can temporarily place food. But sometimes you want a charry crust on a steak or peppers, so you place the food as close to the flame as possible.

If the recipe doesn't specify closing the lid at any point while cooking, you can assume the lid should remain open.

Here are ways to manage the fire.

### CHARCOAL GRILL

To decrease the distance between the food and the heat, place more charcoal, several bricks, or a few pieces of wood in the bottom of the charcoal grill so that the glowing coals are closer to the grill rack. To increase the distance between the food and the heat source in a charcoal grill, create an indirect fire, with the coals to one side.

To adjust the temperature on a closed charcoal grill, open the vents wider to raise the temperature and narrow the vents to lower it. Also, using hardwood lump charcoal, especially mesquite, will create a hotter, faster-burning fire than using briquets.

### GAS GRILL

Turn the heat to high to get more of a charry crust and turn a burner off to create a cool zone. To adjust the temperature on a gas grill, simply turn the knobs.

# 1

# BEEF, PORK, AND LAMB

# PERFECTLY GRILLED BURGERS

**SERVES:** 4

Sometimes the simplest things are hard to beat, like a perfectly grilled hamburger. But simplicity involves good ingredients and good technique. First, it is essential to select the right beef. Buy ground meat from a specified cut, like sirloin or chuck, instead of the generic "ground beef." The latter is not necessarily bad, but the quality will vary, since ground beef can come from any part of the animal. Grill with 80 percent lean burgers—the fat cooks out and makes for a juicy burger. The second secret to perfect burgers is to use medium- to medium-high heat, so they don't burn.

.............................................................................................................................

**1.** Fill a charcoal chimney with briquets, set the chimney on the bottom grill grate, and light. When the coals are ready, dump them into the bottom of your grill and spread evenly. For a gas grill, turn to medium.

**2.** Add salt and pepper to the ground chuck and mix well with your hands. Shape the meat into 4 patties of equal size.

**3.** Grill the burgers for 7 minutes on each side.

**4.** Spread mayonnaise on the inside of each bun and top with a grilled burger. Garnish with the onion slices and enjoy.

1 pound (453.5 g) ground chuck

Salt and freshly ground black pepper to taste

Mayonnaise

4 whole wheat or sourdough buns

4 slices onion, preferably Texas Sweet or Vidalia

Four 8-ounce (227 g) ribeye, sirloin, T-bone, or strip steaks, cut 1 inch (2.5 cm) thick, at room temperature

Fine sea salt and freshly ground black pepper

1 stick (½ cup [112 g]) unsalted butter (optional), melted

1 lemon (optional), quartered

# DIRTY STEAK

**SERVES:** 4

Dwight Eisenhower wasn't the first or only cook to grill steaks directly on hot coals, but he was the most famous one to do it. One of many stories about Ike in the Eisenhower Library archives relates that he liked 3-inch (7.5 cm)-thick beef strip steaks—also called New York strip, shell steak, or Kansas City strip—completely covered with salt and pepper, then placed directly on white-hot coals for a rare, charry-crusted steak that can be addictive. Sorry, gas grillers, but no dirty-steak cooking on your grill—you need the coals for this one.

**1.** Sprinkle both sides of the steaks liberally with salt and pepper. Set aside.

**2.** Fill a charcoal chimney with briquets, set the chimney on the bottom grill grate, and light. When the coals are ready, dump them into the bottom of your grill. Cover half of your bottom grate with briquets.

**3.** When the briquets are white-hot, place each steak directly onto the hot coals using long-handled tongs or a fork. Leave the steaks on the coals for 2 minutes. Turn them over and grill for another 2 to 3 minutes for rare (125°F [52°C] on a meat thermometer). For medium-rare (135°F [57°C]) to medium (140°F [60°C]), leave the steaks on the coals for 1 to 2 minutes longer. Remove the steaks from the coals and brush off the ashes. Spread the melted butter over the top and add a squeeze of lemon before serving, if you desire.

# KISS OF SMOKE RIBEYES, SIRLOIN, STRIPS, OR T-BONES WITH BACON BLUE CHEESE TOPPING

**SERVES:** 4

If you love your juicy steak with good grill marks and the heady aroma of smoke, then this recipe is for you. The olive oil slather keeps the steak from drying out and sticking to the grill grate, a hot fire ensures good grill marks, a cooler zone helps manage flare-ups, and wood chips scattered on the coals (or placed in a metal container near the heat source on your gas grill) provide the smoke. To make your grilled steak even better, anoint it with blue cheese, bacon, and scallions at the end. For this recipe, it's best to have the steaks at room temperature before cooking them; cold steaks take much longer to cook.

.............................................................................................................

**1.** To make the bacon blue cheese topping, in a medium-size bowl with a fork, stir together the blue cheese, buttermilk, bacon, scallion, and Worcestershire sauce. Set aside to use as a garnish for the steaks.

**2.** Mix the olive oil, pepper, and salt together in a bowl and slather the mixture with your fingers onto both sides of each steak.

**3.** Fill a charcoal chimney with briquets, set the chimney on the bottom grill grate, and light. When the coals are ready, dump them into the bottom of the grill, banking them on one side. This will make a cooler space on the grill in order to move the steaks away from direct heat if flare-ups get out of control. For a gas grill, turn to medium-high and keep one burner on low or off.

**4.** To get a hint of smoke, toss ½ cup (45 g) dry wood chips of your choice on the coals, or place a metal container with 1 cup (90 g) dry wood chips near a burner on a gas grill. (It might take up to 20 minutes for the wood chips to start smoldering on a gas grill; the closer you can safely put them near a burner, the quicker they smolder.)

## BACON BLUE CHEESE TOPPING

1 cup (120 g) crumbled blue cheese

¼ cup (60 ml) buttermilk

3 strips hickory-smoked bacon, cooked until crisp and chopped into small pieces

1 scallion (white part and some of the green), chopped

1 teaspoon Worcestershire sauce

¼ cup (60 ml) extra-virgin olive oil

2 teaspoons freshly ground black pepper

1 teaspoon sea salt

Four 8-ounce (227 g) ribeye, sirloin, T-bone, or strip steaks, cut 1 inch (2.5 cm) thick, at room temperature

½ to 1 cup (45 to 90 g) dry pecan wood chips or other hardwood chips

**5.** When you see smoke coming from the wood chips, place the steaks on the grill grate directly over the coals or burners and close the lid for 2 minutes. Open the lid, turn the steaks, and continue grilling and turning every 2 minutes until done to your liking—6 minutes total for rare (125°F [52°C] on a meat thermometer), 8 minutes for medium-rare (135°F [57°C]), and 10 minutes for medium (140°F [60°C]). For a smokier flavor, keep the grill lid closed between turnings. If you get a flare-up during grilling, move the steak to the cooler side of the grill for a minute or so, then move it back over higher heat until done. Serve each steak with the blue cheese topping.

## SRIRACHA MARINADE

⅓ cup (80 g) sriracha sauce

⅓ cup (75 g) Thai sweet chili sauce

⅓ cup (80 ml) soy sauce

2 teaspoons toasted sesame oil

2 to 3 cloves garlic, minced or crushed

1 flank steak (about 1½ pounds [680 g])

# RED ROOSTER FLANK STEAK

**SERVES:** 4

The marinade for this recipe is sometimes called "red rooster sauce" because of the rooster on the label of one of the best-selling brands of sriracha sauce. It works with almost anything, from pork to chicken to tofu. That said, it's particularly well suited to beef. It will flavor a flank steak to perfection, even when there's not much time to marinate; it can work its magic in as little as an hour. Cook to medium-rare, slice the meat in thin slices on the bias, and you'll have a table full of happy eaters.

**1.** Combine all the marinade ingredients in a 1-gallon (3.8 L) zipper-top plastic bag. Add the flank steak to the marinade, seal the bag, and squish it around to coat the steak all over. Refrigerate for at least 1 hour and up to a few hours longer if possible.

**2.** Fill a charcoal chimney with briquets, set the chimney on the bottom grill grate, and light. When the coals are ready, dump them into the bottom of the grill and spread evenly. For a gas grill, turn to medium-high.

**3.** Place the flank steak on the grill directly over the heat and grill with the lid open for about 24 minutes total for medium-rare, turning every 4 minutes or so.

**4.** Transfer to a platter and let stand, loosely tented with aluminum foil, for 5 to 10 minutes. Carve into slices and serve.

# GRILLED FLANK STEAK IN CUMIN–CITRUS MARINADE

**SERVES:** 4

Flank steak, unlike ribeye, is tough and lean. It is less expensive, however, and it takes well to a citrus marinade and medium-high grilling. This great marinade helps turn any tough meat tender and flavorful. The marinating technique also works with boneless pork chops and chicken. Serve this with Stir-Grilled Farmers' Market Vegetables (page 101), which you can grill right along with the steak. Your guests will savor the steak and vegetable combo straight from the grill.

......................................................................................................................

**1.** Combine the marinade ingredients in a bowl and mix well. Put the steak into a gallon (3.8 L)-size zipper-top plastic bag; pour the marinade into the bag over the steak. Seal the bag and marinate the steak overnight in the refrigerator until ready to grill.

**2.** Fill a charcoal chimney with briquets, set the chimney on the bottom grill grate, and light. When the coals are ready, dump them into the bottom of your grill. For a gas grill, turn to medium-high.

**3.** Grill the steak, turning every 3 minutes, until rare (125°F [52°C] on a meat thermometer), about 22 minutes. Set the steak aside to rest for 10 minutes, then cut into thin slices across the grain. Serve with stir-grilled vegetables, if you like.

**CUMIN–CITRUS MARINADE**

1 cup (284 g) frozen orange juice concentrate, thawed

1 cup (235 ml) freshly squeezed lemon juice

1 tablespoon (10 g) granulated garlic

1 tablespoon (7 g) ground cumin

1 teaspoon freshly ground black pepper

½ teaspoon sea salt

2 pounds (907 g) flank steak

## SALSA VERDE

4 to 5 cups (240 to 300 g)
fresh flat-leaf parsley

4 to 6 cloves garlic,
to your taste, peeled

Juice of 1 lemon, with
some of the pulp if you
can coax it out

2 tablespoons (17 g)
capers, drained

2 teaspoons anchovy paste
(optional)

½ cup (120 ml) olive oil

2 to 3 pounds (907 to 1,361 g)
London broil, ribeye, or
flat iron steaks, cut 1 to
1½ inches (2.5 to 3.75 cm)
thick (usually 2 steaks)

Olive oil

Kosher salt and freshly ground
black pepper to taste

# STEAK WITH SALSA VERDE

**SERVES:** 4 to 6

Think Italian, not Mexican, for this salsa verde. This pureed green sauce from Italy is a veritable flavor explosion, the perfect complement to a big grilled steak.

London broil, tenderloin, New York strip, ribeye, and flat iron steaks all work with this recipe. Carving the steak into fairly thin slices will help make up for the relative toughness of these cuts. Just be sure to carve the steaks on the bias (at a slight angle) and keep the slices thin, about ¼ to ⅜ inch (6.5 to 9.5 mm) thick. Top with the salsa verde, and you've got quite a meal.

........................................................................................................................................

**1.** Combine the salsa verde ingredients in a food processor or blender and blend until the sauce has the consistency of a milkshake. Because of the salty nature of the capers and anchovies, no additional salt is needed. Pour the sauce into a bowl, cover, and refrigerate until needed.

**2.** Fill a charcoal chimney with briquets, set the chimney on the bottom grill grate, and light. When the coals are ready, dump them into the bottom of the grill and spread evenly. For a gas grill, turn to high.

**3.** Coat the steak evenly with the olive oil; dust with salt and pepper.

**4.** Sear the steak over the hot fire with the lid open for 10 minutes total, 5 minutes per side.

**5.** Move the steaks away from the hottest coals or the lit burners and cook them with the lid down for an additional 4 to 6 minutes total for rare to medium-rare.

**6.** Transfer the steak to a platter and let stand, loosely tented with aluminum foil, for about 10 minutes. Carve into slices and top with the salsa verde.

# PORTERHOUSE FOR TWO WITH CAMBOZOLA BUTTER

**SERVES:** 2

When you're in the mood for something over the top, you should try this. Cambozola is a German cheese, something of a cross between a blue cheese and a brie. If you cannot find it, just substitute a brie or a blue cheese.

The Cambozola butter can be served as is right from the bowl. For a more formal presentation, place the butter on a piece of plastic wrap, shape into a log, wrap tightly, refrigerate, and cut into rounds before serving.

Think of a porterhouse steak as an oversized T-bone steak, cut much thicker and composed of two steaks (one on either side of the bone): a tenderloin steak and a New York strip (or Kansas City strip). The presence of the bone makes the steaks particularly flavorful and succulent.

........................................................................................................................

**1.** About an hour before serving, combine the Cambozola butter ingredients in a medium-size bowl and mix thoroughly with a fork. Set aside to allow the flavors to mellow.

**2.** Fill a charcoal chimney with briquets, set the chimney on the bottom grill grate, and light. When the coals are ready, dump them into the bottom of the grill and spread evenly. For a gas grill, turn to high.

**3.** Rub the steak with the olive oil. Sprinkle liberally with salt and pepper. Sear the steak over the hot fire with the lid open for 10 to 12 minutes total, 5 to 6 minutes per side.

**4.** Transfer to a platter and let stand, loosely tented with aluminum foil, for about 5 minutes. Serve topped with as much of the Cambozola butter as desired.

## CAMBOZOLA BUTTER

5 ounces (142 g) Cambozola cheese

10 tablespoons (140 g) European-style butter, at room temperature (regular salted butter can be substituted, but try to find this type of butter if you can)

4 to 5 large cloves garlic, crushed

1 tablespoon (14 g) anchovy paste

1 porterhouse steak (1½ to 2 pounds [680 to 907 g]), 1½ inches (3.75 cm) thick

1 tablespoon (15 ml) olive oil

Kosher salt and freshly ground black pepper to taste

# FLORENTINE PORTERHOUSE STEAK ON A TUSCAN HEARTH GRILL

**SERVES:** 4

Four 8-ounce (227 g) porterhouse steaks, cut 3 inches (7.5 cm) thick

Extra-virgin olive oil

Sea salt and freshly ground black pepper to taste

A cast-iron Tuscan grill is a great way to convert your fireplace hearth into a place to grill. This is especially fun and dandy on harsh winter days. Since steaks from Italian Chianina cattle are not available in most American supermarkets, here's a recipe for grilling a porterhouse steak in the Florentine style. You can also grill this on a charcoal or gas grill outside, over high heat. Serve this steak with a traditional Tuscan side dish of warm cannellini beans (opposite).

........................................................................................................................

**1.** Place the cast-iron Tuscan grill in your fireplace. Fill a charcoal chimney with briquets or hardwood charcoal and light. When the coals are ready, dump them into the bottom of your hearth, about 3 inches (7.5 cm) under the grate of the Tuscan grill.

**2.** Brush the steaks with olive oil. Place the steaks on the grill grate. After 7 minutes turn the steaks over and lightly salt the crusty side. After another 7 minutes turn the steaks over and lightly salt that side. Remove the steaks and sprinkle lightly with pepper and more olive oil before serving. The steaks will be crusty on the outside and rare (125°F [52°C] on a meat thermometer) on the inside. Add more minutes on the grill for your desired level of doneness.

# TUSCAN BEANS

**SERVES:** 4

Two 15-ounce (425 g) cans cannellini beans, drained

½ teaspoon freshly ground black pepper

½ teaspoon fine sea salt

Zest of 1 lemon

1 tablespoon (15 ml) freshly squeezed lemon juice

1 tablespoon (15 ml) extra-virgin olive oil

Rosemary sprigs for garnish

......................................................

**1.** Combine the beans, pepper, salt, lemon zest, lemon juice, and olive oil in a medium-size saucepan. Heat over medium heat for about 5 minutes and serve alongside the steak, with a sprig of rosemary for garnish. These can also be served cold as a bean salad, if you prefer.

4 full slabs baby back ribs

1 cup (192 g) Rendezvous or other dry barbecue seasoning, plus more for "dry" ribs

1 cup (235 ml) cider vinegar for "dry" ribs

Bottled barbecue sauce of your choice for "wet" ribs

# RENDEZVOUS-STYLE BABY BACK RIBS

**SERVES:** 4

When you want to grill ribs, tender baby backs are your choice. Charlie Vergos, founder of the Rendezvous Restaurant in Memphis, Tennessee, has sold boxcar loads of grilled baby backs to enthusiastic rib eaters since 1948. Now, his kids run the Rendezvous while Charlie's legacy lives on. The Rendezvous sells ribs "wet," with Charlie's liquid barbecue sauce, or "dry," covered with a special mix of dry seasonings.

When slow-smoking ribs, it's good to remove the membrane from the back of the slab. But when grilling, leave it on, because the fire tends to shrivel the membrane away from the meat, making its removal unnecessary.

For Rendezvous-style baby back ribs, choose the special Rendezvous seasoning (available at hogsfly.com), a mild chili powder, or a dry rub that you like—it's the seasoning that gives ribs their signature flavor. Serve these ribs with doctored-up coleslaw: Add chopped sweet red and yellow bell peppers to a bag of prepared coleslaw and mix it in a bowl with your favorite vinaigrette or creamy dressing.

**1.** Sprinkle both sides of each slab with the seasoning and set aside.

**2.** Fill a charcoal chimney with briquets, set the chimney on the bottom grill grate, and light. When the coals are ready, dump them into the bottom of the grill and spread evenly. For a gas grill, turn to medium.

**3.** Grill the whole slabs, turning every 5 minutes, until done, about 45 minutes. The ribs are done when the meat pulls away from the ends of the bones. Just before serving "dry" ribs, sprinkle or spray the cooked ribs with the vinegar and add more dry seasoning. To make "wet" ribs, brush the cooked ribs with barbecue sauce.

# BARBECUED COUNTRY-STYLE PORK RIBS

**SERVES:** 4 to 6

These succulent, meaty cuts of pork are the essence of simplicity to grill, but they satisfy the burliest of appetites. Just don't overcook them, please! Remember, the USDA says that you only have to cook pork to 160°F (71°C) for it to be safe to eat. Keep your instant-read thermometer at the ready and take the ribs off the grill as soon as they reach the magic temperature. You'll be amazed at the difference it makes when you don't overcook pork.

Country-style ribs are cut from the sirloin or rib end of the pork loin and are known as the meatiest of all pork ribs—the kind you need a knife and fork to eat. Baby back ribs can be prepared the same way, but the bone-to-meat ratio is far greater.

Letting the ribs "marinate" with the dry rub for 2 hours will produce a good result, but letting them sit in the refrigerator overnight does remarkable things for the flavor.

3 to 4 pounds (1.3 to 1.8 kg) country-style pork ribs

Kosher salt and freshly ground black pepper to taste

Your favorite dry rub (or make your own using the recipe on the opposite page)

Barbecue sauce of your choice

**1.** Sprinkle the ribs liberally with salt, pepper, and dry rub. Place the ribs in a large zipper-top plastic bag and refrigerate for at least 2 hours and preferably overnight.

**2.** Fill a charcoal chimney with briquets, set the chimney on the bottom grill grate, and light. When the coals are ready, dump them into the bottom of the grill and spread evenly. For a gas grill, turn to medium-low.

**3.** Arrange the ribs so they are not directly over the hottest coals or a burner. Close the lid and cook for 35 to 45 minutes total, turning every 12 minutes or so, until the internal temperature reaches 150°F (66°C) (it will continue to rise as the meat rests).

**4.** Swab the ribs all over with barbecue sauce. Close the lid and allow the ribs to cook for 3 or 4 minutes more before serving.

## BARBECUE-STYLE DRY RUB

¼ cup (57.5 g) paprika

2 tablespoons (20 g) kosher salt

2 tablespoons (15 g) chili powder

2 tablespoons (14 g) ground cumin

2 tablespoons (30 g) dark brown sugar

1 tablespoon (13 g) granulated sugar

1 tablespoon (6 g) freshly ground black pepper

1 tablespoon (6 g) freshly ground white pepper

1 tablespoon (4 g) dried oregano

2 teaspoons cayenne pepper, or to taste

.............................................................

**1.** Combine the ingredients in a small bowl. Store any leftover rub in an airtight jar, preferably in the freezer.

## DIJON MASCARPONE

1 cup (240 g) mascarpone

⅓ cup (80 g) Dijon mustard

½ cup (142 g) frozen apple juice concentrate, thawed

⅓ cup (16 g) finely chopped fresh chives

1 bone-in pork loin roast (3 to 4 pounds [1.3 to 1.8 kg])

1 tablespoon (15 ml) vegetable oil

Kosher salt and freshly ground white pepper to taste

Finely chopped fresh chives for garnish

# PORK LOIN WITH DIJON MASCARPONE

**SERVES:** 6

Pork has long been paired with slightly sweet, fruity sauces or marinades. This sauce, a combination of mascarpone cheese, Dijon mustard, and apple juice concentrate, follows that tradition but breaks some new ground at the same time.

For some reason, a lot of home cooks shy away from grilling larger cuts of meat. In essence, the technique is no different from that of grilling a steak; these larger cuts just take longer to cook. Presented on a platter, right off the grill, a pork loin is an impressive sight, always sure to elicit plenty of oohs and aahs. For the roast to be at its succulent best, be sure to let it rest under a loose tent of aluminum foil for 10 minutes or so before carving. This resting step holds true for any large cut of meat.

......................................................................................................................................

**1.** Combine the Dijon mascarpone ingredients in a medium-size bowl. Cover and refrigerate until needed.

**2.** Fill a charcoal chimney with briquets, set the chimney on the bottom grill grate, and light. When the coals are ready, dump them into the bottom of the grill and spread evenly. For a gas grill, turn to medium.

**3.** Rub the pork roast with the vegetable oil; dust with salt and pepper.

**4.** Place the pork roast over the center of the grate and cook, with the lid down, for 1 to 1¾ hours, turning every 20 minutes. With an instant-read thermometer, start checking the temperature at the center of the roast after 1 hour. The roast is perfectly cooked when the internal temperature reaches 150°F to 155°F (66°C to 68°C) (the temperature will continue to rise while the meat rests).

**5.** Transfer the roast to a platter and let stand, loosely tented with aluminum foil, for 10 minutes. Carve the roast and serve with a dollop of the sauce on top of each portion. Garnish with chopped chives.

# BARBECUE-GLAZED PORK CHOPS AND STEAKS

**SERVES:** 4

Many backyard cooks are famous for their grilled pork chops. St. Louis pitmasters are famous for their grilled pork *steaks*. The technique is the same whether grilling chops or steaks—an indirect fire (meaning coals or burners medium-high on one side, low on the other), with barbecue sauce brushed on during the last minutes of grilling for a glazed, not burned, finish. For flavorful and juicy steaks or pork chops, use cuts at least 2 inches (5 cm) thick.

....................................................................................................

**1.** Combine the glaze ingredients in a bowl. Mix well and set aside.

**2.** Brush the pork with the olive oil, then season with the salt and pepper.

**3.** Fill a charcoal chimney with briquets, set the chimney on the bottom grill grate, and light. When the coals are ready, dump them into the grill and spread them evenly over half of the bottom grate. For a gas grill, turn to medium-high, with one burner on low or off. Place the chops or steaks over direct heat and grill, turning occasionally, for 10 minutes or until almost done. If fat flares up or the meat begins to burn, move it to the cooler part of the grill for a few minutes. Brush the pork chops or steaks with the glaze and grill for another 5 minutes, until the sauce sets into a smooth sheen.

### BARBECUE GLAZE

1 cup (250 g) KC Masterpiece Classic Blend barbecue sauce or other tomato-based barbecue sauce (you could use Maull's, in honor of St. Louis)

1 tablespoon (13 g) turbinado sugar

1 tablespoon (15 ml) cider vinegar

Four 8-ounce (227 g) pork chops or steaks, at least 2 inches (5 cm) thick

4 tablespoons (60 ml) extra-virgin olive oil

1 teaspoon sea salt

1 tablespoon (6 g) freshly ground black pepper

## USING GRILLING SAUCES

Homemade and commercially available grilling sauces are meant to add a glazed surface and extra seasoning to grilled foods. Since the glaze is composed mostly of sweeteners such as sugar, corn syrup, honey, or molasses, which tend to burn, apply the sauce during the last few minutes of grilling. This way, you avoid burning the sauce and your meat will look nicely glazed instead of charred.

One 16-ounce (475 ml) bottle creamy-style French dressing

6 cloves garlic (optional), minced or crushed

1 tablespoon (3 g) crumbled dried rosemary or 1 teaspoon minced fresh rosemary (optional)

1 leg of lamb (about 4 pounds [1.8 kg]), boned and butterflied

# DRESSED-UP BUTTERFLIED LEG OF LAMB

**SERVES:** 6 to 8

Butterflying a leg of lamb is rather challenging, and I wouldn't recommend it for most home cooks. Have your butcher do it for you, and if you really want to curry their favor, order it a day ahead, as it takes some time to do it properly—even for an experienced butcher.

**1.** Pour the French dressing (and garlic and rosemary, if using) into a 1-gallon (3.8 L) zipper-top plastic bag. Add the lamb and refrigerate for at least 4 hours, and preferably overnight.

**2.** Fill a charcoal chimney with briquets, set the chimney on the bottom grill grate, and light. When the coals are ready, dump them into the bottom of the grill and spread evenly. For a gas grill, turn to medium.

**3.** Place the lamb over the center of the grill grate and cook, with the lid down, for 50 to 60 minutes total, turning every 12 to 15 minutes, until an instant-read thermometer reads 140°F (60°C) for medium-rare.

**4.** Transfer to a platter and let stand, loosely tented with aluminum foil, for about 10 minutes. Cut into slices and serve.

# 2

# CHICKEN AND DUCK

# THREE SATAYS

**EACH SATAY SERVES:** 4 to 6

If you have the time, marinate these satays overnight before cooking them: The more intense the flavor, the better. There are three variations here—chicken, beef, and pork—each with its own marinade. All of them are winners and perfect as predinner small bites. Preparation and cooking techniques are the same for all three. If you're using bamboo skewers, don't forget to soak them first.

......................................................................................................

**1.** Put the meat strips in a quart (946 ml)-size zipper-top plastic bag. (Use a separate bag for each type of meat, if you're making more than one type.)

**2.** Mix all the ingredients for the marinade or marinades in small bowls or cups, then pour the designated marinade or marinades over the meat, seal the plastic bag or bags, and squish around to coat the strips. Let marinate in the refrigerator for at least 2 hours and preferably overnight.

**3.** Fill a charcoal chimney with briquets, set the chimney on the bottom grill grate, and light. When the coals are ready, dump them into the bottom of the grill and spread evenly. For a gas grill, turn to medium.

**4.** Remove the meat from the bag and thread the strips on skewers, accordion-style.

**5.** Place the skewers on the racks and grill, with the lid up, for a total of 10 minutes, 5 minutes per side. You may want to have a thin-bladed spatula on hand when it comes time to flip the satays. Use it upside down, sliding the blade gently under the meat to loosen it from the grill. Serve hot or at room temperature.

## CHICKEN SATAY

1 pound (453.5 g) boneless, skinless chicken breast, cut into ⅜-inch (9.5 mm)-thick slices

## BEEF SATAY

1 pound (453.5 g) beef (top round, sirloin, flank, or other steak), cut into ⅜-inch (9.5 mm)-thick slices

## PORK SATAY

1 pound (453.5 g) boneless pork chops, cut into ⅜-inch (9.5 mm)-thick slices

## GINGER–GARLIC MARINADE

¼ cup (60 ml) sake

¼ cup (60 ml) soy sauce

1 tablespoon (6 g) finely chopped fresh ginger

2 to 3 cloves garlic, finely chopped or crushed

¼ cup (25 g) chopped scallions

### PEANUT–SESAME MARINADE

½ cup (120 ml) soy sauce

¼ cup (65 g) creamy
peanut butter

1 tablespoon (15 ml)
toasted sesame oil

1 tablespoon (15 ml) hot sauce
of your choice

### HOISIN–CHILI MARINADE

¼ cup (60 ml) soy sauce

¼ cup (62.5 g) hoisin sauce

¼ cup (56 g) Thai sweet
chili sauce

1 tablespoon (15 ml)
vegetable oil

## MUMBO RUB

2 tablespoons (12 g) freshly ground black pepper

1 teaspoon sea salt

1 teaspoon granulated garlic

1 tablespoon (7 g) paprika

6 pounds (2.7 kg) chicken wing drums

## MUMBO SAUCE

½ cup (120 g) ketchup

½ cup (120 ml) cane syrup or (101 g) turbinado sugar

1½ tablespoons (25 ml) distilled white vinegar or sweet or dill pickle juice

2 tablespoons (30 ml) hot sauce (such as Gator Hammock, Texas Pete, or Louisiana)

### NOTE

When serving hands-on saucy foods such as this, give each guest a damp washcloth.

# GRILLED CHICKEN WING DRUMS WITH MUMBO RUB AND SAUCE

**SERVES:** 4

Grilling bone-in chicken pieces sprinkled with a rub and brushed with a barbecue sauce is easy if you use the right technique—turn, turn, turn! Otherwise, it's burn, burn, burn! Drums are the meatiest part of the wing and are readily available. If you want to make this recipe with legs and thighs, just follow the same format but grill them 10 to 15 minutes longer. Cane syrup is available at specialty markets, some grocery stores, or online—it's a dark, licorice-tasting syrup used in Creole and Caribbean cooking.

**1.** Combine the rub ingredients in a bowl. Put the drums in a zipper-top plastic bag, add the rub, seal the bag, and shake until the drums are coated with seasoning. Refrigerate overnight.

**2.** Combine the sauce ingredients in a saucepan. Stir while the sauce simmers for 5 minutes over medium heat. Set aside to pour over the grilled drums or to serve on the side for dipping.

**3.** Fill a charcoal chimney with briquets, set the chimney on the bottom grill grate, and light. When the coals are ready, dump them into the bottom of your grill and spread evenly. For a gas grill, turn to medium-high.

**4.** Grill the drums, turning frequently with long-handled tongs, for 15 to 20 minutes, until done. Brush with the mumbo sauce during the last minutes of grilling or remove the drums to a bowl or platter and cover with the mumbo sauce. Serve immediately.

# THUNDER THIGHS

**SERVES:** 4 or 5

This very simple recipe could easily give the ubiquitous buffalo wings a run for their money. As any old-time cook will tell you, "The closer to the bone, the sweeter the meat." For that reason, this recipe calls for bone-in thighs. The presence of the bone really does add flavor to the finished product. Skin-on thighs—even if you're planning to eat them without the skin—are best: The skin helps keep the chicken moist and succulent while grilling.

**1.** Combine all the marinade ingredients in a 1-gallon (3.8 L) zipper-top plastic bag.

**2.** Rinse the chicken thighs in cold water. Pat dry, place in the bag with the marinade, and refrigerate for 1 to 3 hours.

**3.** Fill a charcoal chimney with briquets, set the chimney on the bottom grill grate, and light. When the coals are ready, dump them into the bottom of the grill and spread evenly. For a gas grill, turn to medium.

**4.** Place the chicken thighs on the grill grate, offset a little bit from the hottest part of the coals or burners. Cook, with the lid down, for a total of about 40 minutes, turning every 10 minutes.

**5.** Transfer to a platter and let stand, loosely tented with aluminum foil, for 10 minutes. Serve hot.

## SRIRACHA MARINADE

½ cup (120 ml) soy sauce

½ cup (156 g) sriracha sauce

1 teaspoon toasted sesame oil

3 to 4 cloves garlic, finely minced or crushed

8 to 10 skin-on, bone-in chicken thighs

2 tablespoons (3.5 g) fresh rosemary leaves, minced

2 tablespoons (5 g) fresh sage leaves, minced

2 cloves garlic, minced

Juice of 1 lemon

1 tablespoon (6 g) freshly ground black pepper

1 teaspoon sea salt

One 4-pound (1.8 kg) roasting chicken, backbone removed and flattened

1 cup (235 ml) extra-virgin olive oil for basting and drizzling, divided

2 clean red-clay paver bricks (available at hardware or home improvement stores), wrapped well in aluminum foil

Fresh lemon wedges for garnish

# TUSCAN SPATCHCOCK CHICKEN GRILLED UNDER BRICKS

**SERVES:** 4

"Spatchcock" is a technique in which the chicken is cut down the middle and the backbone removed so that the two attached halves can be grilled flat on the grate. Either remove the backbone of the chicken and flatten it yourself, or have your butcher do it. The technique of placing the foil-covered bricks on the flattened chicken keeps more of its surface on the grill for better caramelization. This method works for any small to medium-size whole bird, from quail to Cornish game hens to a small turkey.

**1.** Combine the rosemary, sage, garlic, lemon juice, pepper, and salt in a bowl. Lift portions of the chicken skin, making small cuts if necessary, and put pinches of the herb mixture beneath the skin. Refrigerate the chicken for an hour, allowing time for the meat to absorb the flavors.

**2.** Fill a charcoal chimney with briquets, set the chimney on the bottom grill grate, and light. When the coals are ready, dump them into the bottom of the grill and spread evenly. For a gas grill, turn to medium.

**3.** When your fire is ready, brush the chicken all over with some of the olive oil and place on the grill. Press the bricks onto the flattened chicken. Every 7 to 10 minutes, remove the bricks (wearing your welder's gloves to avoid burning your hands), then turn and baste the chicken with the olive oil (use about ½ cup [120 ml] for basting). Grill for 30 minutes, or until a knife inserted in the meatiest portion of the thigh produces clear juice or a meat thermometer inserted in the thigh registers 160°F (71°C). To serve, drizzle with the remaining ½ cup (120 ml) olive oil and accompany with lemon wedges.

# CHICKEN BREASTS WITH CHÈVRE AND YELLOW PEPPER PUREE

**SERVES:** 4

This dish is easy to prepare but still falls into the "fancy" category. The flavors are so special and fresh that diners can't help but sit up and take notice. Yellow bell peppers have a unique, delicious flavor. If you have any sauce left over, it's great on pasta.

........................................................................................................................

1. Fill a charcoal chimney with briquets, set the chimney on the bottom grill grate, and light. When the coals are ready, dump them into the bottom of the grill and spread evenly. For a gas grill, turn to medium-high.

2. Place the whole peppers on the grill directly over the heat. Cook the peppers for about 20 minutes total, turning them every 5 minutes or so, until completely charred on all sides.

3. Place the peppers in a doubled paper grocery bag and tightly fold over the top. Allow the peppers to steam in the bag for 10 minutes.

4. Using a sharp paring knife, remove the stems, seeds, and skins from the peppers and discard. In a blender, combine the roasted peppers, olive oil, vinegar, basil, and salt. Blend on low speed until smooth. Pour the pepper puree into a bowl and reserve until needed.

5. Coat the chicken breasts with oil; dust with salt and pepper. Place the chicken breasts on the grill, offset a little bit from the hottest parts, skin side up. Cook, with the lid down, for a total of 8 to 12 minutes, 4 to 6 minutes per side, or until the juices run clear when the breasts are pierced with the tip of a sharp knife.

6. Cut the goat cheese into ⅜-inch (9.5 mm)-thick rounds. Carve the chicken breasts into ⅜-inch (9.5 mm)-thick slices. On a serving platter, alternate slices of chicken with slices of cheese. Top with the yellow pepper puree and serve immediately.

3 large yellow bell peppers

2 tablespoons (30 ml) olive oil

1 tablespoon (15 ml) sherry vinegar

6 large fresh basil leaves

¼ teaspoon kosher salt

4 boneless, skin-on chicken breast halves (about 2 pounds [907 g] total)

1 tablespoon (15 ml) olive oil

Kosher salt and freshly ground black pepper to taste

One 8-ounce (227 g) log plain goat cheese

## ORANGE-MAPLE SYRUP SAUCE

Juice of 2 freshly squeezed oranges

Zest of 1 orange

½ cup (120 ml) pure maple syrup

4 boneless, skinless chicken breast halves, halved lengthwise to make 8 pieces

3 tablespoons (45 ml) extra-virgin olive oil

1 tablespoon (2.4 g) fresh thyme leaves

Sea salt and freshly ground black pepper to taste

Fresh orange slices for garnish

# FLASH-GRILLED CHICKEN BREASTS WITH ORANGE-MAPLE SYRUP SAUCE

**SERVES:** 4

The better quality the chicken, the tastier the result. Flash grilling means you grill fast over higher heat—easy to do if you halve the chicken breasts lengthwise and then flatten them to a ½-inch (1.25 cm) thickness before grilling. Steamed or grilled buttered fresh asparagus or broccoli and a crisp white California or New York wine are good complements. Flash grilling works well for any thin, boneless piece of meat—veal, pork, beef, or lamb.

**1.** Combine the sauce ingredients in a bowl. Stir until well blended and reserve for later.

**2.** Brush each breast with the olive oil, followed by a sprinkling of the thyme leaves, salt, and pepper. Put the chicken in a gallon (3.8 L)-size zipper-top plastic freezer bag, press the air out, and seal it. Place on a cutting board and roll a rolling pin over the chicken to flatten to about a ½-inch (1.25 cm) thickness.

**3.** Fill a charcoal chimney with briquets, set the chimney on the bottom grill grate, and light. When the coals are ready, dump them into the bottom of the grill and spread evenly. For a gas grill, turn to medium-high.

**4.** Grill the chicken for 2 minutes; turn over and grill for another 2 minutes. Before turning again, brush the up side with ¾ of the orange–maple syrup sauce, flip, and then brush the other side and grill for 2 more minutes. To test for doneness, cut into the thickest part or test with a meat thermometer (160°F [71°C ] for done, as the temperature will rise 5 degrees after the chicken is removed from the grill). If the chicken is pink or underdone, brush with more finishing sauce and grill another minute on each side. When done, remove the chicken from the grill to a cutting board. Cut lengthwise into ½-inch (1.25 cm) strips and serve immediately with the rest of the sauce. Garnish with fresh orange slices.

# GRILL-ROASTED WHOLE CHICKEN WITH CHEESY CORN AND LIMA BAKE

**SERVES:** 4

One 3- to 4-pound (1.4 to 1.8 kg) fryer chicken

3 tablespoons (45 ml) olive oil

1 teaspoon sea salt

1 tablespoon (6 g) freshly ground black pepper

A grill-roasted whole chicken takes longer to cook than the usual hot and fast grilling of a boneless and skinless breast, but the flavors are fabulous and well worth the effort. The key is grill roasting the chicken indirectly, with coals banked on one side of a charcoal grill or burners turned to medium-high on one side of a gas grill. The chicken sits on the cooler side getting bronzed and plump and juicy. Put the casserole on to grill bake at the same time, and before you know it, dinner's ready!

**1.** Fill a charcoal chimney with briquets, set the chimney on the bottom grill grate, and light. When the coals are ready, dump them into the grill and spread them evenly over half of the bottom grate. For a gas grill, turn to medium-high, with one burner on low or off.

**2.** Brush the chicken with the olive oil and season with the salt and pepper.

**3.** Place the chicken on the indirect (cooler) side of the grill and close the lid. Grill roast for 1½ hours, turning the chicken every 20 to 30 minutes so it browns evenly on all sides. Test for doneness by inserting a knife into the meatiest portion of the thigh. If clear juice runs from the chicken or a meat thermometer inserted in the thigh registers 160°F (71°C) (temperature will rise 5 degrees after the chicken is removed from the grill), the chicken is done. During the last 30 to 45 minutes of grill roasting, put the Cheesy Corn and Lima Bake on to grill bake.

## NOTE

For a kiss of smoke, sprinkle a handful of apple or pecan chips over the coals or place 1 cup (90 g) chips in a metal container near a burner on your gas grill.

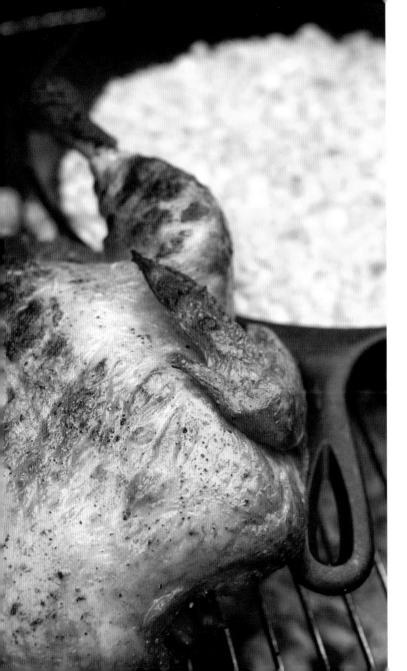

## CHEESY CORN AND LIMA BAKE

**SERVES:** 4

One 12-ounce (340 g) package frozen corn, thawed

One 12-ounce (340 g) package frozen baby lima beans, thawed

8 ounces (227 g) shredded Cheddar cheese

1 cup (235 ml) buttermilk

1 stick (½ cup [112 g]) unsalted butter, melted

2 scallions (white part and some of the green), chopped

1 teaspoon freshly ground black pepper

1 teaspoon sea salt

...........................................................

**1.** Place all the ingredients in a medium-size bowl and mix well.

**2.** Transfer the mixture to a seasoned cast-iron skillet (10¼ inches [26 cm] in diameter × 2 inches [5 cm] deep) or a disposable aluminum pan. Place next to the chicken on the indirect side of the grill, close the lid, and grill bake for 30 to 45 minutes or until browned and bubbling. Serve immediately, using the skillet as the serving dish.

## CITRUS CHUTNEY

1 pink or white seedless grapefruit, peeled and chopped

1 seedless orange, chopped

2 seedless tangerines, chopped

1 lemon, seeded and chopped

1 lime, seeded and chopped

1 cup (202 g) turbinado sugar

½ cup (120 ml) cider vinegar

1 teaspoon fresh ginger, peeled and grated

1 teaspoon sea salt

1 teaspoon prepared horseradish

¼ teaspoon cayenne pepper

½ cup (75 g) golden raisins

½ cup (56 g) pecan pieces

½ cup (75 g) chopped red bell pepper

Four 4- to 5-ounce (113 to 142 g) bone-in duck breasts, rinsed and patted dry

Fine sea salt and freshly ground black pepper to taste

# CRISPY-SKINNED GRILLED DUCK BREAST WITH CITRUS CHUTNEY

**SERVES:** 4

Duck requires special treatment when grilled or barbecued. Successfully grilling a fatty duck breast requires an indirect fire, grilling fat-side down for most of the time, and moving the duck to the cool side of the grill when the inevitable flare-ups occur. The chutney, which can cook on the grill along with the duck, adds a tart contrast to the rich duck. Leave the rinds on the fruits, except for the grapefruit.

**1.** To make the chutney, place the citrus fruits, sugar, vinegar, ginger, salt, horseradish, and cayenne pepper in a blender or food processor. Process the mixture until smooth and pour into a heavy-duty stainless-steel saucepan or a disposable aluminum pan. Add the raisins, pecans, and red bell pepper. Set aside.

**2.** Fill a charcoal chimney with briquets, set the chimney on the bottom grill grate, and light. When the coals are ready, dump them into the grill and spread them evenly over half of the bottom grate. For a gas grill, turn to medium-high, with one burner on low or off.

**3.** Simmer the chutney on the grill over direct heat for 20 minutes and set aside; keep warm.

**4.** Grill the duck breasts fat side down over direct heat, moving frequently. If the flames become too intense, move the duck to the cooler side of the grill, opposite the fire. Resume grilling when the flames subside. After 20 to 30 minutes, when the fat side is blackened and the fat has cooked out, turn the breasts over and grill the meat side for 1 to 2 minutes, or until the duck is medium-rare (135°F [57°C] on a meat thermometer). Remove the duck to a serving platter. Sprinkle each breast lightly with salt and pepper. Serve immediately with the chutney.

# QUARTERED DUCK WITH FIG AND GREEN OLIVE SAUCE

**SERVES:** 4

The rich meat of duck can stand up to a variety of assertive flavors and sauces, such as this delicious fig and green olive combination. Serve this fancy-yet-easy meal when you have company over and stand by for compliments to the chef.

To make preparation easier, ask the butcher to quarter the duck for you. Although grilling duck may be new to you, the technique is basically no different from that of cooking any other fowl. But there is one important fact to note: Duck contains much more fat than chicken (wild ducks are the exception to this rule), and for this reason, grilling the duck indirectly—that is, not over the hottest coals or directly over the gas burners—is a necessity. Cooking it directly over a live fire would produce a conflagration in a matter of minutes.

.......................................................................................................................

**1.** Combine the sauce ingredients in a medium saucepan over medium heat. Allow to come just to a boil. Remove from the heat and set aside.

**2.** Fill a charcoal chimney with briquets, set the chimney on the bottom grill grate, and light. When the coals are ready, dump them into the bottom of the grill and spread evenly. For a gas grill, turn to medium-high.

**3.** Rinse the duck quarters in cold water and blot dry with several thicknesses of paper towel.

**4.** On a gas grill, turn the center burner off and turn the other burners to medium. On a charcoal grill, distribute the coals around the perimeter, leaving the center empty. Position the duck quarters over the center of the grate, skin side up, and grill, with the lid down, for 30 to 40 minutes total, turning every 10 minutes or so. The duck is done when an instant-read thermometer inserted into the thickest part of the thigh registers 180°F (82°C) (don't let the thermometer touch a bone).

**5.** Transfer to a platter and let stand, loosely tented with aluminum foil, for 5 to 10 minutes. Reheat the sauce if necessary. Place duck pieces on individual serving plates and top with the sauce. Serve immediately.

## GREEN OLIVE SAUCE

½ cup (160 g) fig preserves

1 cup (235 ml) tawny port

½ cup (64 g) pitted green olives, halved

¼ teaspoon kosher salt

½ teaspoon freshly ground black pepper

1 duck (4 to 5 pounds [1.8 to 2 kg]), quartered

# 3

# FISH AND SHELLFISH

# SHRIMP WITH BASIL AND PROSCIUTTO

**SERVES:** 4 to 6

16 large raw shrimp, peeled, tails on

16 large fresh basil leaves

16 thin slices prosciutto

1 lemon, cut into wedges

Freshly ground black pepper to taste

This appetizer (or, if you like, a main course for a light dinner or lunch) is a triple threat if ever there was one: three simple ingredients that add up to much more than the sum of their parts. Serve these hot off the grill or at room temperature—they'll disappear so fast it'll make your head spin.

Variations on this recipe include using either sea scallops (not bay scallops, as they are much too small) or calamari, or a combination of any two, or all three! You could also substitute other fresh herb leaves to suit your taste. Whether you are cooking shrimp, scallops, or calamari, keep a very close eye while grilling, as overcooking will make them tough in a matter of just a minute or two. Once the shrimp, scallops, or calamari have turned from translucent to opaque, they will need only a minute or so longer to be cooked to perfection.

**1.** Fill a charcoal chimney with briquets, set the chimney on the bottom grill grate, and light. When the coals are ready, dump them into the bottom of the grill and spread evenly. For a gas grill, turn to medium-low.

**2.** Rinse the peeled shrimp in cold water. Blot dry on several thicknesses of paper towel.

**3.** Wrap each shrimp with a basil leaf, followed by a slice of prosciutto; the natural stickiness of the prosciutto will hold the basil in place.

**4.** Place the wrapped shrimp on the grill over medium-low heat and cook, with the lid up, for a total of 3 minutes, 1½ minutes per side.

**5.** Place the grilled shrimp on a platter; squeeze the fresh lemon juice over them and sprinkle with a few grinds of black pepper. Serve hot or at room temperature.

## HORSERADISH SAUCE

⅔ cup (160 ml) low-fat buttermilk

⅓ cup (75 g) mayonnaise

¼ cup (56 g) prepared horseradish

1 teaspoon sea salt

1 teaspoon Dijon-style mustard

¼ teaspoon cayenne pepper, or to taste

8 wooden or bamboo skewers, soaked in water for at least 4 hours

1 pound (453.5 g) unpeeled shrimp (51 to 60 count)

24 mini bell peppers (orange, red, and yellow), stemmed and seeded, or 4 medium-size bell peppers (orange, red, and yellow), seeded and cut into 1-inch (2.5 cm) strips

3 tablespoons (45 ml) extra-virgin olive oil for brushing or misting

1 teaspoon granulated garlic

1 teaspoon freshly ground black pepper

1 teaspoon sea salt

1 cup (90 g) dry hickory wood chips

# HICKORY–GRILLED SHRIMP SKEWERS WITH HORSERADISH SAUCE

**SERVES:** 4

The trick to grilling food on skewers is to soak the bamboo skewers so they don't burn, thread the shrimp onto the skewers so they touch but are not crowded, then grill until the shrimp are just opaque. Leave the shells on, which protects them from drying out too much. Throwing a handful of hickory chips on the fire gives the shrimp a wonderful smoky aroma. In general, skewers are easy to grill, as long as the pieces of food are roughly equal in size. Although some people don't like to put proteins and vegetables on the same skewer because vegetables get done faster than chicken or beef, there's no worry here because the shrimp cook just as fast as the vegetables.

**1.** Combine the sauce ingredients in a bowl and whisk until blended. Cover and refrigerate until the shrimp is served.

**2.** Thread 3 mini peppers or pepper strips and 2 shrimp onto each skewer, alternating the shrimp and peppers (begin and end with a pepper). Brush or spray with the olive oil, then sprinkle with the granulated garlic, pepper, and salt. If you use this technique for jumbo shrimp, use 2 parallel skewers with each set of shrimp. That way, the jumbos will be easier to turn while grilling.

**3.** Fill a charcoal chimney with briquets, set the chimney on the bottom grill grate, and light. When the coals are ready, dump them into the bottom of the grill and spread evenly. For a gas grill, turn to medium-high. Throw the hickory chips on the hot coals or place them in a metal container near a burner on a gas grill.

**4.** When smoke rises from the wood chips, grill the shrimp skewers. Using long-handled tongs, turn the skewers frequently until done, about 4 minutes. The shrimp will look orange/pink and opaque when done. Overdone shrimp will be tough but still delicious. Serve immediately with individual portions of horseradish sauce on the side.

# MUSSELS BORDELAISE

**SERVES:** 1 per dozen mussels

Mussels make a great appetizer, or you can turn this dish into an entrée with the addition of a crisp green salad and some warm, crusty bread. Actually, even if you're serving this as an appetizer, be sure to provide some good bread for sopping up the delicious juices. Mussel lovers will be able to eat a dozen or more as an appetizer without blinking, so adjust these quantities as needed for your crowd, with a separate foil packet for each dozen mussels. Rinse and debeard the mussels first, discarding any that won't close (a live mussel will slowly close its shell when handled). After cooking, discard any mussels that haven't opened.

12 mussels

⅓ cup (80 ml) dry white wine

1 clove garlic, crushed or minced

Juice of ½ lemon

1 tablespoon (4 g) finely chopped fresh flat-leaf parsley

¼ teaspoon kosher salt

Freshly ground black pepper to taste

**1.** Fill a charcoal chimney with briquets, set the chimney on the bottom grill grate, and light. When the coals are ready, dump them into the bottom of the grill and spread evenly. For a gas grill, turn to medium-high.

**2.** Place the mussels in the center of a rectangle of heavy-duty aluminum foil about 24 inches (61 cm) long. Form into a bowl-like shape and add the white wine, garlic, lemon juice, parsley, salt, and pepper. Fold up the sides of the foil and crimp the top and sides together to make a sealed foil packet.

**3.** Place the foil packet directly on top of the heat and close the lid. Cook for 4 to 5 minutes, by which time the mussels should be open.

**4.** Remove the packet from the grill; open carefully (watch out for steam) and pour the contents into a large shallow bowl. Serve immediately.

12 to 20 large sea scallops

4 to 8 bay leaves, halved

Melted unsalted butter

Salt and freshly ground black pepper to taste

Lemon wedges

# GRILLED SEA SCALLOPS WITH BAY LEAVES

**SERVES:** 4

Bay scallops and sea scallops are two different species of shellfish. In simple terms, sea scallops are much larger than bay scallops: There are anywhere from fifteen to forty sea scallops to a pound (453.5 g), while there are from ninety to one hundred bay scallops to a pound (453.5 g). Easy as this recipe is, it's also elegant and tasty. The flavors of these two ingredients—the scallops and the bay leaves—are highly complementary. Allow three to five sea scallops per person, depending on their size and your diners' appetites. Because their size can vary, watch carefully to prevent overcooking, which results in tough scallops. If using bamboo skewers, soak them in water first.

**1.** Fill a charcoal chimney with briquets, set the chimney on the bottom grill grate, and light. When the coals are ready, dump them into the bottom of the grill and spread evenly. For a gas grill, turn to medium-high.

**2.** Thread 3 to 5 scallops onto 2 parallel skewers (to keep them from spinning around when turning them), alternating each scallop with half a bay leaf. Repeat with the remaining scallops and bay leaves. Liberally brush the skewered scallops with melted butter and dust with salt and pepper.

**3.** Place the skewered scallops on the grill, directly over the heat. Cook, with the lid up, for 6 to 8 minutes total, 3 to 4 minutes per side. The scallops are ready when they turn opaque but are still fairly soft to the touch.

**4.** Serve hot off the grill with lemon wedges.

# GRILL-SEARED SEA SCALLOPS

**SERVES:** 4 as an appetizer, 2 as a main course

Perfectly seared scallops don't have to be a restaurant dish only—you can do these on your grill, too. You'll need a seasoned cast-iron skillet with a griddle topper or a grill pan that you normally use on the stove—the kind that is ridged on one side and flat on the other. You will need to place the skillet or griddle as close to the coals or burners as possible and let it get really hot—hot enough that if you hold your hand about 2 inches (5 cm) from the bottom of the skillet or griddle, you can only leave it there for 3 seconds. One big scallop topped with a squiggle of Mae Ploy Sweet Chili Sauce (a slightly fiery and sweet Asian sauce) makes a great appetizer. Four big scallops with a side dish such as asparagus is a delicious meal. This technique also works for squid, baby octopus, or jumbo shrimp. In addition, it works well for filet mignon—just brush the meat with olive oil, season to taste, and sear for a steakhouse crust.

8 large sea scallops

2 tablespoons (30 ml) extra-virgin olive oil

1/2 teaspoon fine sea salt

1 teaspoon freshly ground black pepper

1/2 teaspoon granulated garlic or more to taste

1 cup (50 g) panko breadcrumbs flavored with honey and butter or plain

Mae Ploy Sweet Chili Sauce for serving (optional)

1. Rinse each scallop under cold running water to remove any excess sand. Pat dry and put in a bowl.

2. Stir the olive oil, salt, pepper, granulated garlic, and panko crumbs together in a separate bowl. Coat the scallops evenly with the mixture and set aside.

3. Fill a charcoal chimney with briquets, set the chimney on the bottom grill grate, and light. When the coals are ready, dump them into the bottom of the grill and spread evenly. For a gas grill, turn to medium-high. Place the skillet or griddle on the grill grate.

4. When the skillet or griddle is very hot (see page 13), place the scallops in the hot pan and sear for 2 minutes on each side. Serve immediately, plain or with a squiggle of chili sauce on each scallop if desired.

## NOTE

You can also put the scallops in a grill basket that's been well coated with olive oil, though you may lose some of the panko coating this way. Grill for 2 minutes on each side.

# TUNISIAN TILAPIA IN PITA

**SERVES:** 4

Tilapia in Tunis? It's not as far-fetched as you might think: Primarily farm-raised in the US, tilapia is native to parts of Africa and the Middle East. Called St. Peter's fish there, tilapia was, during biblical times, common in the Sea of Galilee. When you want a casual, pick-it-up-in-your-hands-and-eat-it dinner that's also a great meal, give this a try. These filled pita sandwiches—with the wonderful garlic-infused yogurt, diced cucumbers, tomatoes, and fresh mint—are excellent paired with a Mediterranean-style salad with crisp greens, crumbled feta cheese, black olives, and a simple vinaigrette. If you use bamboo skewers to grill the fish, soak them in water first.

Tilapia, like sole, flounder, and cod, is a relatively delicate fish and thus can present some grilling difficulties, especially when turning it. If you're concerned about fish breaking apart while you grill it, buy yourself a nonstick metal fish basket with long handles for easy turning. Place the skewers of tilapia in the basket, close it up, and place on the grill. Perfection is guaranteed.

1. Put the yogurt in a small bowl. Add the garlic to the yogurt and mix well. Reserve in the refrigerator until needed.

2. Mix all the ingredients for the rub in a small bowl.

3. Slice the tilapia into strips about ¾ inch (2 cm) wide and 3 to 4 inches (7.5 to 10 cm) long. Put the tilapia slices in a bowl and lightly coat with the vegetable oil.

4. Put one-third of the dry rub into a zipper-top plastic bag. Put half of the tilapia slices in the bag; top with another one-third of the dry rub. Place the remaining sliced tilapia in the bag; sprinkle the remaining dry rub over the top. Seal the bag closed and shake vigorously to coat the fish evenly with the rub.

5. Fill a charcoal chimney with briquets, set the chimney on the bottom grill grate, and light. When the coals are ready, dump them into the bottom of the grill and spread evenly. For a gas grill, turn to medium. Preheat the oven to 250°F (120°C).

## GARLIC–YOGURT SAUCE

8 ounces (227 g) plain yogurt

3 or 4 cloves garlic, minced or crushed

## CORIANDER–CARAWAY RUB

1 tablespoon (6 g) ground coriander

1 teaspoon ground caraway seeds

¼ teaspoon garlic powder

¼ teaspoon cayenne pepper

¼ teaspoon curry powder

¼ teaspoon salt

1½ pounds (680 g) tilapia

1 tablespoon (15 ml) vegetable oil

4 large pita bread rounds

## EXTRAS

1 cucumber, peeled, seeded, and cut into small chunks

Chopped tomatoes

Chopped fresh mint

Hot sauce (preferably harissa)

**6.** Thread the tilapia slices, accordion-style, onto skewers.

**7.** Wrap the pita breads in aluminum foil and place them on the edge of the grill to warm. Place the tilapia skewers on the grill, directly over the hot burners. Grill, with the lid up, for 4 to 6 minutes total, 2 to 3 minutes per side.

**8.** Cut the top quarter from the warm pitas, using scissors or a sharp knife. Fill each pita pocket with the following ingredients, in any order you choose: grilled tilapia, garlic-yogurt sauce, cucumbers, tomatoes, mint, and hot sauce. Serve immediately.

4 tuna steaks (2 to 2½ pounds [907 to 1,134 g] total), 1 to 1½ inches (2.5 to 3.75 cm) thick

1 tablespoon (15 ml) olive oil

Freshly ground white pepper to taste

Sweet paprika to taste

### GREEN OLIVE SAUCE

½ cup (86 g) store-bought green olive tapenade

¼ cup (60 ml) dry white wine

Juice of ½ lemon

2 cloves garlic, crushed

# TUNA STEAKS WITH GREEN OLIVE SAUCE

**SERVES:** 4

The distinctive flavor of grilled tuna is nicely complemented by the equally distinctive flavor of the olive tapenade sauce. If you have a recipe for homemade green olive tapenade, feel free to use it here. Serve this hot off the grill; if there are any leftovers, they'll make a wonderful tuna salad or salade niçoise.

If you are new to grilling fish, a firm-fleshed variety, such as tuna, is the best place to start. Other fish with firm flesh include salmon, swordfish, grouper, halibut, sea bass, and striped bass. Because these varieties tend to firm up even more as they cook, they are easier to handle and turn than more delicate fish such as haddock or tilapia. If the thought of grilling fish still makes you nervous, use a metal fish basket with a long handle for easy turning. Those with nonstick surfaces are best.

**1.** Rinse the tuna steaks in cold water. Blot dry with several thicknesses of paper towel. Coat with the olive oil on both sides; dust with white pepper and paprika.

**2.** Fill a charcoal chimney with briquets, set the chimney on the bottom grill grate, and light. When the coals are ready, dump them into the bottom of the grill and spread evenly. For a gas grill, turn to medium-high.

**3.** While the grill is preheating, in a small saucepan over medium heat combine all the ingredients for the sauce. Bring just to a boil and remove from the heat. Set aside.

**4.** Place the tuna steaks on the grill, directly over the hot burners. Cook, with the lid up, for 6 minutes total, 3 minutes per side, for rare tuna, or increase the cooking time to up to 10 minutes total, 5 minutes per side, for well-done tuna.

**5.** Transfer to a platter and top with the warm olive sauce. Serve immediately.

# GRILLED WHOLE TROUT WITH CORNBREAD STUFFING

**SERVES:** 4

Whole freshwater or ocean fish are delicious when grilled using this simple technique. To avoid the frustration and messiness of fish sticking to the grill, use a grill basket. Oil the basket with olive oil to prevent the fish from sticking to the basket. You'll need two grill baskets for four trout or any similar-sized whole fish that will fit in the grill basket. If you can find young, fresh sardines or mackerel (oily fish that resist sticking), just place them whole on the grill grate, omit the stuffing, and dinner will be ready in no time.

........................................................................................................

**1.** Combine the cornbread stuffing ingredients in a medium-size bowl. Mix well and set aside. Rinse the trout under cold running water and pat dry. Brush the grill baskets and the trout—inside and out—with the olive oil. Stuff each trout with one-quarter of the stuffing. Place 2 trout in each prepared grill basket.

**2.** Fill a charcoal chimney with briquets, set the chimney on the bottom grill grate, and light. When the coals are ready, dump them into the bottom of the grill and spread evenly. For a gas grill, turn to medium-high.

**3.** Grill the fish for 4 minutes on the first side, then turn and grill for another 4 minutes. After that, turn the fish frequently until done, about another 2 minutes on each side. The fish is done when it flakes easily when tested with a fork in the thickest part. Remove from the basket and serve immediately.

## CORNBREAD STUFFING

1½ cups (180 g) dry cornbread crumbs

⅓ cup (34.7 g) chopped scallion (white part and some of the green)

⅓ cup (60 g) fire-roasted red bell peppers, store-bought or homemade (page 86), chopped

One 4-ounce (113 g) can diced green chiles

2 tablespoons (30 ml) extra-virgin olive oil

1 teaspoon freshly ground black pepper

½ teaspoon sea salt

4 whole trout (1½ to 2 pounds [680 to 907 g] each), cleaned

Olive oil for brushing

## LEMON–DILL BUTTER

½ stick (¼ cup [55 g]) unsalted butter, melted

Zest of ½ lemon

1 tablespoon (15 ml) freshly squeezed lemon juice

2 tablespoons (8 g) fresh dill, chopped

2 pounds (907 g) salmon fillets, preferably skin-on

2 tablespoons (30 ml) extra-virgin olive oil

1 teaspoon sea salt

1 teaspoon freshly ground black pepper

# GRILLED SALMON FILLETS WITH LEMON–DILL BUTTER

**SERVES:** 4

Even if a fish fillet's skin has been removed, you can tell which is the skin side and which is the flesh side—the skin side is always slightly darker. But if you can get a fish fillet with the skin on, the grilling is easier, as the skin helps hold the tender fish together. It's also very important to clean and oil your grill grates before grilling the fish to keep the fillet from sticking or tasting like last night's hamburger. Halibut or any firm-fleshed fish fillet is also delicious grilled using this method.

**1.** Combine the lemon-dill butter ingredients in a small bowl, mix well, and set aside. Rub the salmon on both sides with the olive oil and season with the salt and pepper.

**2.** Fill a charcoal chimney with briquets, set the chimney on the bottom grill grate, and light. When the coals are ready, dump them in the bottom of the grill and spread evenly. For a gas grill, turn to medium-high.

**3.** Put the salmon skin side down on the grill grate and close the lid. Grill for 5 minutes, turn the fish using a wide fish spatula or 2 grill spatulas, close the lid, and grill for 5 more minutes. The fish is done when it flakes easily when tested with a fork in the thickest part. Drizzle with lemon-dill butter and serve.

# CEDAR-PLANKED SALMON WITH CHIMICHURRI SAUCE

**SERVES:** 4

If you haven't tried plank grilling and thought it was too complicated, you're in for a treat. Your guests will be wowed by the subtle smoky aroma and cedar wood flavor. You can find nontreated hardwood planks for grilling at hardware, home improvement, grocery, and barbecue stores. Soak the plank in a large plastic garbage bag or in a deep sink, weighted down with a clean brick or canned goods. Use an indirect fire, with the plank on the cooler side. The chimichurri sauce adds a piquant, herbal flavor to the salmon. Feel free to experiment by using this technique with boneless, skinless chicken breasts or other fish fillets such as farm-raised catfish, haddock, halibut, or ocean perch, and/or try other types of hardwood planks—oak, hickory, alder, or maple.

............................................................................................................

**1.** Combine the sauce ingredients in a food processor or blender and process until smooth. Set aside.

**2.** Fill a charcoal chimney with briquets, set the chimney on the bottom grill grate, and light. When the coals are ready, dump them into the grill and spread them evenly across half of the bottom grate. For a gas grill, turn to medium-high with one burner on low or off.

**3.** Remove the plank from the water, pat dry, and rub the side of the plank the salmon will rest on with 1 tablespoon (15 ml) of the olive oil. Rub the remainder of the olive oil on both sides of the salmon. Sprinkle the salmon lightly with salt and pepper and set it on the oiled side of the plank.

**4.** Place the planked salmon on the cooler side of the grill, close the lid, and cook for 20 minutes. Lift the lid and check the salmon for doneness—if the fish begins to flake when tested with a fork in the thickest part, it's done. If it isn't done, put the lid back on the cooker and grill the salmon for another 5 minutes or until done. Serve the salmon drizzled with the chimichurri sauce.

### CHIMICHURRI SAUCE

1 cup (60 g) packed chopped fresh flat-leaf parsley leaves

1 cup plus 2 tablespoons (265 ml) extra-virgin olive oil

⅓ cup (80 ml) cider vinegar

Zest and juice of 1 lemon

2 cloves garlic, minced

¼ teaspoon sea salt, plus a bit more to taste

¼ teaspoon freshly ground black pepper, plus a bit more to taste

1 cedar plank, soaked in water for 4 hours or overnight

One 3-pound (1.4 kg) salmon fillet

# 4

# VEGGIES, FRUIT, AND CHEESE

# FIRE-ROASTED PEPPER SALSA

**MAKES:** about 1 cup (240 g)

Fire-roasted bell peppers make a great appetizer over cream cheese, a delicious side dish, or a complement to grilled steak, chicken, pork, or fish. The trick to getting the peppers really fire-roasted is to have the grill grate as close to the heat source as possible. On a charcoal grill, this means putting something like bricks, hardwood, or more charcoal in the bottom of your grill, so when you dump the coals in, they will sit higher, nearer the grill grate. For a gas grill, just crank it up to high. Turbinado sugar is a light brown, unrefined sugar, sometimes found under the brand name Sugar in the Raw; cane syrup is a thick, sweet syrup used in Caribbean and Creole cooking.

1 red bell pepper

1 orange bell pepper

1 jalapeño chile (optional)

1 scallion (white part and some of the green), chopped

½ cup (101 g) turbinado sugar or (120 ml) cane syrup

2 tablespoons (30 ml) cider vinegar

---

**1.** Place a few bricks, hardwood logs, or about a chimney's worth of charcoal briquets on the bottom of your charcoal grill, leaving some space to set down the chimney starter. Fill the chimney with briquets, set the chimney on the bottom grill grate, and light. When the coals are ready, dump them on top of the bricks, wood, or charcoal. For a gas grill, turn to high.

**2.** Place the peppers (including the jalapeño, if using) over direct heat. Turn them constantly with long-handled tongs, one after the next, for 3 minutes. Remove the peppers from the coals to a brown paper lunch bag to cool for 10 minutes.

**3.** When the peppers are cooled, remove them from the bag. Rinse the peppers under cold running water and dry. Remove and discard the pepper stems, seeds, and any blackened skin that is peeling off. Dice peppers, combine with the remaining ingredients in a bowl, stir together, and eat as you see fit.

6 medium to large tomatoes (preferably ones with relatively flat bottoms, so they'll stand up straight on the grill and on the plate)

Olive oil

Chopped garlic to taste

Salt and freshly ground black pepper to taste

Dried basil, oregano, or rosemary to taste (optional)

# GARLICKY GRILLED TOMATOES

**SERVES:** 6

This recipe is a classic illustration of the less-is-more principle: getting great flavor from a small number of ingredients. Interestingly, heating tomatoes on the grill turns even less-than-stellar specimens into something quite delicious. If you want to try an incredibly easy and tasty pasta sauce, coarsely chop several of the grilled tomatoes and place them in a shallow bowl. Adjust the seasonings to your taste, adding more olive oil, salt, and pepper as desired, and pour the mixture on top of hot cooked pasta, or try it over cooled pasta for a summertime pasta salad. Top with grated Parmesan cheese, if desired.

Another option for grilled tomatoes is to hollow them out and fill the shells with cooked, chopped spinach mixed with chopped garlic to taste and as much crumbled feta cheese as you desire. Cook until the tomatoes begin to sag a little, approximately 6 to 10 minutes over medium heat. It's an excellent combination of flavors that makes a fantastic appetizer.

**1.** Fill a charcoal chimney with briquets, set the chimney on the bottom grill grate, and light. When the coals are ready, dump them into the bottom of the grill and spread evenly. For a gas grill, turn to medium.

**2.** Using a sharp paring knife or a tomato corer, remove the tomato cores, cutting almost but not completely to the bottom. Fill the cavity with a drizzle of olive oil, chopped garlic to taste, salt and pepper to taste, and dried herbs, if using.

**3.** Place the tomatoes on the grill directly over the heat and cook, with the lid down, for 6 to 10 minutes without turning, until the tomatoes start to sag a little—a sure sign that the flesh is thoroughly heated through.

**4.** Carefully transfer to a platter using a wide spatula and serve hot or at room temperature.

# ASPARAGUS WRAPPED IN PROVOLONE AND PROSCIUTTO

**SERVES:** 4 to 6

Any time you wrap food for grilling, it calls for a little extra care in handling it on the grill. You have to keep your wits about you, especially when turning the food. To make the situation less stressful, you can always use a toothpick to keep everything in place—just be sure to remind your diners that the toothpicks are there.

........................................................................................................................

**1.** Bring a large skillet of water to a boil over high heat. Add the asparagus and blanch for 1½ to 2 minutes. Immediately place the blanched asparagus in a large bowl of ice water for about 3 minutes to stop the cooking. Drain and dry on a large kitchen towel or several thicknesses of paper towel. (This is the one time I break my own rule on parboiling vegetables.)

**2.** Fill a charcoal chimney with briquets, set the chimney on the bottom grill grate, and light. When the coals are ready, dump them into the bottom of the grill and spread evenly. For a gas grill, turn to medium-low.

**3.** Place a slice of prosciutto on the work surface and lay an asparagus spear on top of one end of the prosciutto. Place a piece of provolone next to the asparagus spear. Tightly wrap the prosciutto around the asparagus and cheese in a spiral fashion; the prosciutto will hold the cheese in place. Repeat with the remaining prosciutto, asparagus, and cheese.

**4.** Place the asparagus on the grill grate and cook, with the lid up, for a total of 5 to 6 minutes, 2½ to 3 minutes per side.

**5.** Place the grilled asparagus on a platter. Drizzle the sherry vinegar over the top and sprinkle on some black pepper. Serve hot or warm.

12 fat spears fresh asparagus, bottoms trimmed, tough skins from bottom half peeled with a vegetable peeler

12 long, thin strips prosciutto, about as wide as the asparagus

12 long, thin strips provolone cheese, about as wide as the asparagus

2 tablespoons (30 ml) sherry vinegar

Freshly ground black pepper to taste

2 large heads escarole

2 tablespoons (30 ml) sherry vinegar

Salt and freshly ground pepper to taste

# GRILLED WHOLE ESCAROLE

**SERVES:** 4

Botanically, escarole and endive are one and the same, known in Latin as *Cichorium endivia*. The difference between them is in the way they are grown: Escarole is raised for its broad outer leaves; endive is the center portion of the plant, usually pale in color. Both forms have a slightly bitter taste that many people find appealing. Grilling whole heads of escarole results in a slight smokiness that really complements the flavor of the escarole. Dressed with a little sherry vinegar, salt, and pepper, grilled escarole becomes a complex combination of tastes—not to mention very nutritious.

The first time you do this, it may seem a little horrifying, as it's practically impossible not to burn some of the outside edges of the leaves. Not to worry: The burnt edges are easily cut off with a pair of scissors, leaving behind the slightly smoky, steamed escarole. You can experiment with other whole heads of leafy greens using this same technique. Just be sure they go on the grill with some water still clinging to them.

......................................................................................................................................

**1.** Fill a charcoal chimney with briquets, set the chimney on the bottom grill grate, and light. When the coals are ready, dump them into the bottom of the grill and spread evenly. For a gas grill, turn to medium-low.

**2.** Wash the escarole thoroughly under plenty of cold water. Do not dry it; the extra water will help keep the outer leaves from burning.

**3.** Place the escarole directly over the heat. Cook, with the lid down, for 8 minutes total, turning after 4 minutes, until some of the outside leaves are browned and the whole head of escarole starts to turn a bit limp.

**4.** Transfer the escarole to a cutting board. If any of the ends of the escarole leaves are burnt, simply cut them off with scissors or scrape them off with the edge of a sharp butcher knife. Chop the escarole coarsely, discarding the stem end, and dress with sherry vinegar and salt to taste. Serve hot or at room temperature.

# LIME-AND-CHILE-GRILLED CORN ON THE COB, TWO WAYS

**SERVES:** 4 to 6

Grilled corn on the cob is a classic favorite complement to all grilled meats, and it's easy to prepare. Try both of these techniques to see which one you like best—shucked corn will have grill marks on the corn kernels and more flavor of the grill; corn grilled in the husk will be more tender and moist. Choose the sweetest variety of corn you can find.

.......................................................................................................................

**1.** Combine the lime-chile butter ingredients in a 10 × 13-inch (25.5 × 33 cm) disposable aluminum pan or one large enough to hold all the ears of corn.

**2.** For shucked corn, remove all leaves and silk and rinse the corn under cold running water. Don't worry if a few silks remain; they will burn off when grilled. For corn grilled in the husk, no preparation is needed.

**3.** Fill a charcoal chimney with briquets, set the chimney on the bottom grill grate, and light. When the coals are ready, dump them into the grill and spread them evenly over half of the bottom grate. For a gas grill, turn to medium-high with one burner off.

**4.** Place the aluminum pan with the lime-chile butter on the cooler side of the grill. Place the corn directly over the heat. Turn constantly with long-handled grill tongs; shucks on the unshucked corn will burn and blacken in places. Shucked corn will be completely cooked in about 10 minutes; unshucked will take about 15 minutes, maybe a bit longer. Test for readiness by checking an ear to see if the kernels are tender. If ready, remove the corn from the grill, shuck if necessary, then place it in the warm lime-chile butter. Turn the corn in the butter to make sure the whole ear is seasoned. Serve on a platter or on individual plates with lime wedges.

## LIME-CHILE BUTTER

1 stick (½ cup [112 g] unsalted butter, melted

½ teaspoon sea salt

1 teaspoon freshly ground black pepper

1 teaspoon mild or hot chili powder

Lime juice to taste

6 ears fresh corn

Fresh lime wedges for garnish

1 large eggplant, about
1 pound (453.5 g)

Extra-virgin olive oil

Ground cumin to taste

Juice of ½ lemon

Kosher salt and freshly ground
black pepper to taste

# GRILLED WHOLE EGGPLANT

**SERVES:** 2

Here's a new and really wonderful twist that eggplant lovers will, well, love. It might seem like one of those procedures that you think will never work—but miraculously, it does. This method works best with the standard, large purple eggplants.

The recipe can be embellished by adding ¼ cup (60 g) of tahini, combined with minced garlic to taste, to the eggplant flesh after grilling. Garnish with chopped fresh flat-leaf parsley and chopped toasted walnuts, and you've got a version of the wonderful Middle Eastern dip baba ghanoush, to serve with warm slices of pita bread. Outstanding.

**1.** Fill a charcoal chimney with briquets, set the chimney on the bottom grill grate, and light. When the coals are ready, dump them into the bottom of the grill and spread evenly. For a gas grill, turn to medium.

**2.** Place the eggplant on the grill directly over the heat and cook, with the lid down, for 20 or 30 minutes, turning every 5 minutes. The eggplant will puff up like a balloon during grilling.

**3.** Transfer the eggplant to a cutting board. Poke a hole or two in the eggplant skin with the tip of a sharp knife. The eggplant will deflate. Set aside to cool slightly.

**4.** When the eggplant is cool enough to handle, cut it in half with a sharp knife. Using a spoon, scrape the soft flesh away from the skin. Put the flesh in a bowl. Drizzle with extra-virgin olive oil, a dusting of cumin, the lemon juice, and salt and pepper to taste. Serve warm or at room temperature.

# GRILLED ZUCCHINI WITH HERBS

**SERVES:** 2 to 4

You can never have too many good zucchini recipes, because there are times, like late summer, when most gardens produce more zucchini than anyone knows what to do with. This recipe is a big hit with everyone who tries it. Maybe it's the surprise of eating zucchini that has been cut into strips instead of rounds, which seems to make the squash taste better. Try this with any variety of summer squash or similar medium-firm vegetable, like cucumbers or large white mushrooms.

...........................................................................................................

**1.** Fill a charcoal chimney with briquets, set the chimney on the bottom grill grate, and light. When the coals are ready, dump them into the bottom of the grill and spread evenly. For a gas grill, turn to medium.

**2.** Trim the ends from the zucchini and then slice them lengthwise about ¼ inch (6.5 mm) thick. Drizzle 1 tablespoon (15 ml) of the olive oil on both sides of the zucchini slices.

**3.** Position the zucchini slices on the grill grate, offset a little from the hottest parts of the fire, close the lid, and cook the zucchini for about 2 minutes per side, just long enough to produce grill marks; the zucchini should still have some crunch to it when you remove the slices from the grill.

**4.** Transfer the zucchini to a large bowl, add the remaining olive oil, the lemon juice, and vinegar, and toss gently to combine. Top with the herbs and dust with salt and pepper. Serve hot or at room temperature.

4 zucchini (1½ to 2 pounds [680 to 907 g])

¼ cup (60 ml) olive oil

1 to 2 tablespoons (15 to 30 ml) freshly squeezed lemon juice

1 teaspoon white or red wine vinegar

2 tablespoons (8 g) finely chopped fresh flat-leaf parsley or basil, or a mixture

Kosher salt and freshly ground black pepper to taste

1 pound (453.5 g) zucchini, sliced into ¼-inch (6.5 mm)-thick rounds

1 red bell pepper, sliced lengthwise into ¼-inch (6.5 mm) strips

1 medium-size Vidalia, Texas Sweet, or Walla Walla onion, sliced into ¼-inch (6.5 mm) rings

2 cups (130 g) fresh sugar snap peas

¼ cup (60 ml) extra-virgin olive oil

1 tablespoon (6 g) freshly ground black pepper

1 teaspoon sea salt

# STIR-GRILLED FARMERS' MARKET VEGETABLES

**SERVES:** 4

A grill wok is best for preparing this dish. Use vegetables you like in season, cut into small-enough pieces that they stir grill quickly. Any combo of vegetables of similar size would work, so you could stir grill all summer long and never have the same dish twice! Try zucchini cut into coins, cherry tomatoes, scallions cut into 1-inch (2.5 cm) pieces, small broccoli or cauliflower florets, small green beans—you get the picture.

**1.** Fill a charcoal chimney with briquets, set the chimney on the bottom grill grate, and light. When the coals are ready, dump them into the bottom of the grill and spread evenly. For a gas grill, turn to medium-high.

**2.** Combine all the vegetables in a bowl. Add the olive oil, pepper, and salt, and stir to coat. Transfer to a grill wok.

**3.** Place the grill wok over direct heat. Using wooden paddles or long-handled grill spatulas, stir grill the vegetables until tender-crisp with a little char, 6 to 10 minutes. Serve immediately.

# GRILL-ROASTED FOIL-PACK VEGETABLES

**SERVES:** 4

Root vegetables such as carrots, potatoes, parsnips, onions, and garlic take well to foil-pack grilling. Add a burger or a bratwurst for a complete meal. Experiment with combinations of vegetables, meats, or fruit to develop your own favorites. In general, it's best to stick with vegetables that take about the same time to cook, so don't pair cherry tomatoes with winter squash. But cherry tomatoes with rounds of tender zucchini would be great, and they'd only take 20 minutes. For a wonderful foil pack of fruit, slice up a small peach or nectarine and sprinkle on 1 cup (145 g) of blueberries; dot with butter, sprinkle with brown sugar and cinnamon, close the packet, and grill for about 20 minutes. To adjust the temperature on a charcoal grill, open the vents wider to increase the temperature and narrow the vents to decrease it. For a gas grill, simply turn the knob to medium-high.

........................................................................................

2 large carrots, halved lengthwise

4 small unpeeled red or yellow potatoes, halved

2 small unpeeled sweet potatoes, cut lengthwise into 1-inch (2.5 cm)-thick strips

1 tablespoon (15 ml) extra-virgin olive oil

1 teaspoon freshly ground black pepper

½ teaspoon sea salt

**1.** Fill a charcoal chimney with briquets, set the chimney on the bottom grill grate, and light. When the coals are ready, dump them into the bottom of the grill and spread evenly. For a gas grill, turn to medium-high.

**2.** Place the vegetables into a medium-size bowl. Add the olive oil, pepper, and salt and toss well. Set aside.

**3.** Cut 2 sheets of heavy-duty aluminum foil into 12 × 24-inch (30.5 × 61 cm) pieces. Fold each piece of foil in half. Arrange the vegetables on one piece of the folded foil. Cover the vegetables with the second sheet of foil. Fold and crimp all 4 sides of the foil to seal the vegetables inside.

**4.** Place the vegetable packet over direct heat. Close the lid and adjust the grill temperature to 400°F (204°C) using a thermometer stuck into one of the vent holes in the grill lid. Cook the packet for 1 hour or longer, until the potatoes are tender.

## NOTE

........................................

To make this for a crowd, simply make more packets. Smaller packets are easier to handle, and the food grills faster.

1 small acorn squash, peeled, seeded, and cut into ½-inch (1.25 cm)-thick rings

1 large sweet potato, cut lengthwise into ½-inch (1.25 cm)-thick strips

**CINNAMON BUTTER**

½ stick (¼ cup [55 g]) unsalted butter, melted

1 teaspoon turbinado or light brown sugar

1 teaspoon ground cinnamon

# GRILLED SQUASH AND SWEET POTATOES WITH SWEET CINNAMON BUTTER

**SERVES:** 4

When the leaves begin to turn and fall, don't forget your grill! These autumn vegetables need a quick zap in the microwave to parcook, then you can finish on the grill, complete with a cinnamon-sugar butter. Sweet potatoes and winter squash have more sugars than white potatoes and seem to blacken or dry out faster on the grill, but if you parcook them first in the microwave, they'll grill perfectly. They're delicious with turkey or pork.

**1.** Put the squash and sweet potato on a ceramic plate, cover with a paper towel, and microwave for 4 minutes.

**2.** Combine the cinnamon butter ingredients in a medium-size bowl and set aside.

**3.** Fill a charcoal chimney with briquets, set the chimney on the bottom grill grate, and light. When the coals are ready, dump them into the bottom of the grill and spread evenly. For a gas grill, turn to medium-high.

**4.** Grill the squash and sweet potato for 2 to 3 minutes on each side, until tender and with good grill marks. Remove to a serving plate, spoon the butter mixture over the squash and sweet potato, and serve.

# HERB-GRILLED POTATOES

**SERVES:** 4

The easiest way to grill potatoes is with a square- or rectangular-shaped grill basket. In this recipe, fresh herbs warmed by the grill lend a wonderful flavor to the potatoes. You can also herb grill by placing fresh woody herb branches (rosemary, thyme, or lavender) directly on the hot coals in a charcoal grill or in a metal container near a burner on a gas grill. To substitute sweet potatoes or winter squash, parcook the vegetables first in the microwave until about half done, then finish on the grill. Herb grilling tastes best with vegetables, fish, lamb, or chicken.

.......................................................................................................

**1.** Fill a charcoal chimney with briquets, set the chimney on the bottom grill grate, and light. When the coals are ready, dump them into the bottom of the grill and spread evenly. For a gas grill, turn to medium.

**2.** Oil a grill basket and arrange the potatoes in it with a rosemary sprig on top of each half. Lock the basket and spray or brush the potatoes and rosemary with the olive oil, then season with salt and pepper.

**3.** Grill the potatoes over direct heat, turning frequently, for 20 to 30 minutes, depending upon the thickness of potatoes, until a knife inserted in the thickest part of a potato goes in easily. Remove the rosemary and serve.

4 large baking potatoes, halved lengthwise

8 large fresh rosemary sprigs

¼ cup (60 ml) extra-virgin olive oil or canola oil

Fine sea salt and freshly ground black pepper to taste

## NOTE

.......................................

To add a kiss of smoke to the already grilled potatoes, make an indirect fire by pushing the coals to one side in a charcoal grill or turning one burner off on a gas grill. Transfer the grill basket to the cooler side, sprinkle a handful of water-soaked wood chips on the coals or place a metal container containing 1 cup (90 g) of dry wood chips close to a burner on a gas grill and close the lid for 15 minutes.

4 medium to large russet
potatoes

About ¼ cup (60 ml) olive oil

Salt and freshly ground
black pepper to taste

2 teaspoons crushed dried
rosemary (optional)

# SIMPLE GRILLED POTATO WEDGES

**SERVES:** 4

These are really delicious—basically like big French fries, only much better for you. They are excellent as a side for grilled steaks or fish. Once you've mastered the technique of grilling regular potatoes, you can move on to other hard-fleshed vegetables like winter squash, beets, sweet potatoes, parsnips, and rutabagas. Back in the Pilgrim era, these vegetables, which could be kept over the winter, were sometimes cooked by burying them in live coals. By grilling them, you are continuing a long tradition, and a delicious one at that. With any of the above-mentioned vegetables, choose the largest ones you can find. They all can be cooked the same basic way as white potatoes: Wash, cut into quarters, dry, and then brush with oil. You can grill them directly over the fire, like the potatoes, or simply place them at the edges of the cooking grate while you're grilling something else, turning every 10 minutes or so; they're done when you can insert the tip of a sharp knife easily into the flesh.

**1.** Fill a charcoal chimney with briquets, set the chimney on the bottom grill grate, and light. When the coals are ready, dump them into the bottom of the grill and spread evenly. For a gas grill, turn to medium.

**2.** Cut each potato lengthwise into 4 to 6 wedges and pat them dry with paper towels. In a large bowl, toss the potato wedges with the olive oil and sprinkle with salt, pepper, and the rosemary, if using.

**3.** Place the potato wedges on the grill directly over the heat and cook, with the lid down, for 20 to 30 minutes total, turning every 5 to 7 minutes. The potatoes are ready when the tip of a sharp knife pierces all the way through easily. Serve hot off the grill.

# CARAMELIZED FRUIT KABOBS

**SERVES:** 4

Apples, peaches, and plums all work beautifully for these kabobs, but almost any fruit can be grilled with great success: pears, pineapple, even bananas (leave the skin on and expect it to turn black in the grilling process). In all cases, favor fruit that is on the firm side of ripe, as it will hold up on the grill much better than fruit that is fully ripe and softer. The heat of the grill will help intensify the sugars and bring out the flavors in even less-than-ripe fruits. This combination of fruit is wonderful warm off the grill—kind of like a pie without the crust.

2 small apples

3 or 4 firm, ripe plums

2 or 3 firm, ripe peaches

½ stick (¼ cup [55 g]) unsalted butter, or more as needed, melted

¼ cup (50 g) sugar, or more as needed

**1.** Fill a charcoal chimney with briquets, set the chimney on the bottom grill grate, and light. When the coals are ready, dump them into the bottom of the grill and spread evenly. For a gas grill, turn to medium.

**2.** Cut all the fruit into 1- to 1½-inch (2.5 to 3.75 cm) chunks (rather than wedges). Combine the butter and sugar in a bowl and mix well. Thread the fruit chunks onto skewers, then brush them liberally with the sugared butter.

**3.** Position the skewered fruit over on the grill grate, offset a little from the most intense heat. Close the lid and cook the fruit skewers for 6 to 10 minutes, turning them occasionally, until the fruit begins to soften.

**4.** Serve the fruit warm off the grill.

8 bamboo skewers, soaked in water for at least 4 hours

4 unpeeled ripe bananas, ends trimmed and cut into 2-inch (5 cm) chunks

1 fresh pineapple, peeled, cored, and cut into 2-inch (5 cm) chunks

**LEMONADE GLAZE**

½ cup (101 g) turbinado sugar or ⅓ cup (80 ml) cane syrup

Zest and juice of ½ lemon

# GRILLED PINEAPPLE AND BANANAS WITH LEMONADE GLAZE

**SERVES:** 4

Use gas or hardwood charcoal when grilling fruits. Fruits absorb too much smoke flavor when grilled over wood or briquets. The trick to grilling fruit is to use fruits that are ripe but not overripe or too soft, then brush them with a glaze to bring out the sweetness. Turbinado is a natural, unrefined sugar; you can find that and cane syrup (a thick, sweet syrup used in Caribbean and Creole cooking) at specialty markets, some grocery stores, or online. When you're grilling fruit and using a sugary glaze, it's most important to start out with a clean, oiled grill grate so the fruit is less likely to stick or taste of previously grilled foods.

.........................................................................................................................................

**1.** Make a lengthwise slice on the skin of each unpeeled banana chunk to allow easy peeling after the bananas are grilled. Thread the fruit onto the skewers, alternating chunks of banana and pineapple.

**2.** To make the glaze, put the sugar in a stainless-steel saucepan and cook over medium-high heat until it becomes liquid, about 3 minutes. Stir with a wooden spoon and add the lemon juice and zest. If using cane syrup, simply add the lemon juice with zest and stir, without heating. Set aside.

**3.** Fill a charcoal chimney with hardwood lump charcoal, set the chimney on the bottom grill grate, and light. When the coals are ready, dump them into the bottom of the grill and spread evenly. For a gas grill, turn to medium-high.

**4.** Brush the skewered fruits with the glaze. Place the skewers over direct heat. Grill for 3 minutes on each side, until the fruit is browned. Remove from the grill and brush again with the glaze. Serve immediately.

# CLASSIC BRUSCHETTA

**SERVES:** 8

As simple as it is, bruschetta is one of the most satisfying of all foods to grill—as long as you use good bread, that is. A dense, crusty loaf made in the Italian or French style is what you want. This makes a perfect warm-weather appetizer and is always excellent eating.

Just about every culture has its version of bread-based snacks, whether it's Indian naan, Mexican tortillas, or Middle Eastern pita; interestingly, they all benefit from toasting, especially over a live fire. As simple as the combinations may be—grilled naan and mint chutney, crisp tortillas and guacamole, warm pita and baba ghanoush—they are among the most satisfying things to eat in the culinary universe.

Loaf of dense, crusty Italian or French bread, about 16 inches (40.5 cm) long

Extra-virgin olive oil

About 4 cloves garlic, halved

16 slices fresh tomato (optional)

Shaved Parmesan cheese or 16 small slices fresh mozzarella cheese (optional)

16 fresh basil leaves (optional)

......................................................................................................................................

**1.** Fill a charcoal chimney with briquets, set the chimney on the bottom grill grate, and light. When the coals are ready, dump them into the bottom of the grill and spread evenly. For a gas grill, turn to medium-low.

**2.** Using a serrated knife, cut the bread into slices about 1 inch (2.5 cm) thick. Some folks brush the bread with olive oil before grilling, and others add it after the bread has been toasted. Believe it or not, it makes a difference. Try a couple of slices—one each way—to see which method you prefer.

**3.** Place the bread slices on the grill and cook them, with the lid up, turning once to toast both sides. Watch like a hawk; toasting the slices to golden perfection will take only a couple of minutes.

**4.** While the bread is still warm, rub the top surface with a cut clove of garlic. Top with fresh tomato slices, Parmesan or mozzarella cheese, and/or a few fresh basil leaves, if desired.

1 loaf coarse-textured Italian or French bread (such as a bâtard), about 16 inches (40.5 cm) long

½ pound (227 g) chunk Pecorino Sardo, Asiago, fontina, or Gruyère cheese (listed in order of my preference)

About ¼ cup (60 ml) extra-virgin olive oil

Honey, preferably with a strong floral or herbal flavor

# DESSERT BRUSCHETTA WITH CHEESE AND HONEY

**SERVES:** 8

If you want to end a meal with something that isn't heavy or too sweet, try this. It's a very Mediterranean approach to dessert, perfect for al fresco dining. The crunchiness of the bread, the saltiness of the cheese, and the sweetness of the honey, all bound together with the lusciousness of the olive oil, make for an outstanding combination of flavors. Start with the ingredients given and then branch out, experimenting with other cheeses (such as Camembert, manchego, and feta) and types of honey (such as orange blossom, chestnut, buckwheat, and clover). It won't be long before you come up with your own "house specialty" version of this unusual but satisfying dessert. Use a loaf of bread with a wide diameter—a baguette would be too skinny for this preparation.

**1.** Fill a charcoal chimney with briquets, set the chimney on the bottom grill grate, and light. When the coals are ready, dump them into the bottom of the grill and spread evenly. For a gas grill, turn to medium-low.

**2.** Cut the bread into ¾-inch (2 cm)-thick slices and slice the cheese ¼ inch (6.5 mm) thick.

**3.** Place the bread on the grill grate, offset a little from the highest heat. Toast on one side, with the lid up, for 2 to 3 minutes, checking frequently to avoid burning. Turn the bread, drizzle olive oil generously on the toasted sides, and top each piece with a slice of cheese. Close the lid and continue to cook the bread until the cheese melts (this should only take a couple of minutes).

**4.** As soon as the cheese has melted, transfer the bruschetta to a platter and drizzle with honey. Serve immediately.

# PLANKED GOAT CHEESE WITH SUN-DRIED TOMATO AND BASIL PESTO

**SERVES:** 4

Plank grilling is an easy technique used to enhance the flavor of many foods. The technique is to expose the goat cheese briefly to fire, smoke, and wood, just long enough to combine a smoke accent with the aromatic flavor of the plank, and then complement the cheese with the fresh-from-the-garden flavor of pesto. You can buy untreated hardwood planks at hardware, barbecue, home improvement, and grocery stores. Soak the plank in a large plastic garbage bag or in a deep sink, weighted down with a clean brick or canned goods. This method also works with other soft or semisoft cheeses such as cream cheese, Brie, Camembert, or even Gouda (remove the rind from the Gouda first).

....................................................................................................................

**1.** To make the sun-dried tomato and basil pesto, pour the boiling water over the sun-dried tomatoes in a small bowl and set aside to soften for 15 minutes. Drain, then place the softened sun-dried tomatoes, garlic cloves, basil leaves, Parmesan cheese, parsley, wine, and salt and pepper in a food processor or blender and pulse until blended. Set aside.

**2.** Fill your charcoal chimney with briquets, set the chimney on the bottom grill grate, and light. For a gas grill, turn to medium. Remove the plank from the water, shake off excess water, and wipe both sides of the plank with a dry paper towel. Rub the olive oil on one side of the plank.

**3.** When the coals are ready, dump them into the bottom of your grill and spread evenly. Place the plank, oiled side up, directly on the grill grate over the coals or gas burners. Place the cheese in the center of the plank. Close the grill lid and leave the plank and cheese alone for 15 to 20 minutes or until the cheese has bronzed and has a good, smoky aroma.

## SUN-DRIED TOMATO AND BASIL PESTO

6 ounces (170 g) dry-packed sun-dried tomatoes

3 cups (705 ml) boiling water

2 large garlic cloves, halved

1 cup (24 g) fresh basil leaves, or ½ cup (130 g) basil pesto

½ cup (50 g) freshly grated Parmesan cheese

⅓ cup (20 g) fresh flat-leaf parsley leaves

⅓ cup (80 ml) dry red or white wine

Sea salt and freshly ground black pepper to taste

1 cedar plank, soaked in water for at least 4 hours or overnight

1 teaspoon extra-virgin olive oil, for oiling plank

11 ounces (312 g) fresh goat cheese

¼ cup (30 g) toasted pine nuts or walnut pieces, for garnish

Whole-grain crackers or baguette slices for serving

**4.** Remove the plank from the grill with welder's gloves. Leave the cheese on the plank and put the plank on a platter, wooden cutting board, or dampened hand towel. Top the cheese with ⅓ cup (87 g) of sun-dried tomato and basil pesto and garnish with toasted walnuts or pine nuts. Serve with whole-grain crackers or baguette slices.

## NOTE

You will have about 1 cup (260 g) of pesto left over from this recipe. Freeze it for later use on goat cheese or pasta.

Six 12-inch (30.5 cm)
flour tortillas

3 cups (360 g) shredded
cheese of your choice, such
as Cheddar, Monterey Jack,
or a Mexican blend

Shredded lettuce (optional)

Diced tomatoes and onions
or pico de gallo (optional)

Guacamole (optional)

Hot sauce of your choice
(optional)

# GRILLED QUESADILLAS

**SERVES:** 6

This is an interesting variation on quesadillas. The combination of
crispy flour tortilla and melted cheese with fresh ingredients like lettuce,
tomatoes, and onions is a winner.

If you want to make these more substantial and serve them as a main
course, any type of leftover meat can be added when you add the lettuce.
Crumbled, cooked hamburger or sausage, chopped grilled chicken, or
diced cooked pork are all good possibilities.

To serve, cut the quesadillas into wedges with a sharp knife, like a pizza.
Serve with a variety of your favorite hot sauces or salsas.

**1.** Fill a charcoal chimney with briquets, set the chimney on the bottom
grill grate, and light. When the coals are ready, dump them into the
bottom of the grill and spread evenly. For a gas grill, turn to medium.

**2.** Working with the lid open, place the tortillas directly over the heat
(you may have to cook them in batches). Place ½ cup (58 g) shredded
cheese on one half of each tortilla. Fold the other half over the cheese
and press down slightly. Cook for 2 to 3 minutes, then turn and grill for
another 2 to 3 minutes. Continue cooking, flipping every 2 minutes or
so, until the cheese is completely melted and the tortilla just begins
to brown.

**3.** Remove from the grill and open the folded tortilla carefully. Fill
with shredded lettuce, diced tomatoes and onions (or pico de gallo),
guacamole, and hot sauce as desired. Refold the tortilla, slice into
wedges, and serve immediately.

# INDEX

# ALSO AVAILABLE

Smoking

978-0-7603-9745-9

Rice Cooker

978-0-7603-9741-1

Air Fryer

978-0-7603-9743-5